THE MARK OF THE SPIRIT?

A Charismatic Critique of the 'Blessing' Phenomenon

For Sue

Some friends play at friendship but a true friend
sticks closer than one's nearest kin.
(Proverbs 18:24 NRSV)

THE MARK OF THE SPIRIT?
A Charismatic Critique of the 'Blessing' Phenomenon

EDITED BY
Lloyd Pietersen

First published in 1998 by Paternoster Press

04 03 02 01 00 99 98 7 6 5 4 3 2 1

Paternoster Press is an imprint of Paternoster Publishing,
P.O. Box 300, Carlisle, Cumbria, CA3 0QS, U.K.
http://www.paternoster-publishing.com

British Library Cataloguing in Publication Data
A catalogue record for this book is available from the British Library.

ISBN 0 85364 861 1

Cover design by Mainstream, Lancaster
Typeset by WestKey Ltd, Falmouth, Cornwall
Printed in Great Britain by Mackays of Chatham PLC, Kent

Contents

Preface

This book is a collaborative effort in every way. Whilst each author is ultimately responsible for his or her own work each paper was read, discussed and critiqued in a suitably collegial manner by all four of us at regular meetings conducted at my house. We owe so much to so many people for their influence on our lives either directly through their love, friendship and intellectual stimulation or indirectly through their writings. In particular we would like to thank Peter Fenwick for his initial encouragement to write this book and for his courage to stand up for his convictions which has been a continual inspiration to us. We would also like to thank my wife Sheila for keeping us well fed and watered during our regular get-togethers!

John Lyons adds the following personal acknowledgements:

> Perhaps most of all, I need to acknowledge the help and support I received from Lloyd, Viv and Mark, our meetings providing an oasis of truly Christian calm during my struggles with the rhetoric of the 'Toronto Blessing'; I really don't know what I would have done without you all. My wife, Katie, also deserves my most grateful thanks for her continuous encouragement and strength in what proved a difficult experience for us both. Those who know her well know what a steadfast friend she is. With us along the way were our good friends John Bocking, Rosie Brown, Carl and Sandy Chapman, Tim and Anne Dawson, Graham and Anne Jones, Nicola Le Vallois, Linda Norris, and Scott and Michelle Windle; each of whom in their own way exemplifies the questing nature of the walk of the Christian, despite the pain it has brought some of them. Never

stop asking questions, my friends. But since the Academy has also proved a source of support it is fitting that I should record that debts which can never be repaid are owed to my colleagues and friends Andy (and Tanya) Reimer, Mark (and Lisa) Blackwell, and Robby (and Angela) Waddell. Finally, I would like to thank the Revd Mark Cockayne of St Polycarp's church, Malin Bridge, Sheffield, for doing so much to restore my faith in the leaders of the Charismatic Church.

I too would like to add some personal acknowledgements. I would like to thank Neil and Zoe Edbrooke for their love and friendship, their refreshing refusal, as leaders in a charismatic church, to be swayed by triumphalistic rhetoric and for their amazing ability to embrace those whose perspective on charismatic Christianity may be very different from theirs. Special thanks are due to Peter and Linda Lyne who first took me under their wing and to Tony Pullin for encouraging my teaching role within the local church. My doctoral supervisor, Dr Loveday Alexander, has been a continual source of encouragement to me as has her colleague in the Department of Biblical Studies at the University of Sheffield, Dr Meg Davies. I have really appreciated Alan and Ellie Kreider's obvious concern for the church, their passionate commitment to Christ and the love and care they have shown to me and my family. I can never repay the debt I owe my wife Sheila whose love and support have been consistent and indefatigable through all the struggles I have had with current charismatic praxis. She has constantly demonstrated the meaning of true faithfulness. My children Beth, Keren, Kezi and Jed too have had to put up with dad's continual comments on the 'Toronto Blessing' so much so that they could probably write their own book on the subject! Finally, I want to express my thanks to Sue Roberts who, more than anyone else, has restored my faith in friendship. She has consistently proved what it means to be a true and faithful friend and so, with heartfelt gratitude, I dedicate this book to her.

Lloyd Pietersen
Bristol

Acknowledgements

M. Stibbe, *Times of Refreshing: A Practical Theology of Revival for Today,* p. 72, 109f., published in 1995 by Marshall Pickering, London and reprinted by permission of Harper Collins.

R.P. Martin, *2 Corinthians*, Word Biblical Commentary 40, p. 341, published in 1986 and reprinted by permission of the publishers, Word Publishing, Dallas.

P.F. Esler, *The First Christians in their Social Worlds*, pp. 42–43, published in 1994 and reprinted by permission of the publishers, Routledge, London.

G. Coates, 'Being Yourself', *Fulness* 12, pp. 4–6, reprinted with the permission of Gerald Coates.

G. Perrins, *Fulness* 12, p. 3, reprinted by permission of Gerald Coates.

D. Hervieu-Léger, 'Present-Day Emotional Renewals: The End of Secularization or the End of Religion?', in William H. Swatos, Jr. (ed.), *A Future for Religion: New Paradigms for Social Analysis*, pp. 129–148, copyright 1993, Sage Publications, and reprinted by permission of the publisher, Sage Publications Inc., London.

R. Richter, ' "God is not a Gentleman": The Society of the Toronto Blessing', Stanley Porter and Philip Richter (eds.), *The Toronto Blessing – or is it?*, p. 34, published 1995 and copyright by Darton, Longman and Todd, London and reprinted by permission of the publisher.

Jonathan Edwards, 'The Distinguishing Marks of a Work of the Spirit' both in *Jonathan Edwards on Revival* published in 1994 and reprinted by permission of the publisher Banner of Truth, London.

John Stott, *Acts,* The Bible Speaks Today, p. 118, publisher in 1990 and reprinted by the permission of the publisher, IVP, Leicester.

L.T. Johnson, *Acts,* Sacra Pagina series, vol. 5, p. 103, published in 1992, © by The Order of St. Benedict Inc. Published by the Liturgical Press, Collegeville, Minnesota. Used with permission.

G. Berkouwer, *The Providence of God. Studies in Dogmatics,* pp. 50–124, published in 1952 and reprinted by permission of the publishers, Eerdmans, Grand Rapids.

Introduction

The phenomenon which has come to be known as the 'Toronto Blessing' has been around since 1994. In that time it has swept through a significant number of churches in Britain and elsewhere. As a result some large claims have been made for the Blessing. The contributors to this volume are unconvinced by such claims. We recognize that a great number of respected church leaders, together with a number of biblical scholars and theologians, have endorsed the movement. We beg to differ and are somewhat bemused that the accusation of 'blasphemy against the Holy Spirit' is being directed in some quarters against those who seek to question the movement. On the other hand, we are equally concerned about claims coming from some who are opposed to the 'Toronto Blessing' that the movement is demonic. Such pejorative language, in our view, is decidedly unhelpful.

This volume is a polemical one; in other words, we are consciously engaging in an argument. In *Times of Refreshing* Mark Stibbe has argued that the Toronto phenomenon is the first sign of a coming 'fourth wave' which will result in global revival.[1] Like Stibbe, the contributors to this book are associated with the Department of Biblical Studies at the University of Sheffield. The arguments he uses raise important issues about the Blessing; consequently, although this book is in effect a reply to his, it is also an assessment of the Blessing as such. We offer these papers in the hope that they will open up a substantive debate on the 'Toronto Blessing', free from the rhetoric of 'blasphemy against

---

[1] M. Stibbe, *Times of Refreshing: A Practical Theology of Revival for Today* pp. 10, 21–9.

the Spirit' on the one hand, and epithets such as 'demonic' on the other. Many books have been published in favour of the Blessing; we believe it is important that volumes such as this one should also be available, so that every Christian has the resources to make an informed decision about its nature.

It has been said that Christians should not engage in public disagreements with each other — such disagreements, it is argued, do not demonstrate Christian love. In the light of such comments, it seems right to offer a brief defence of Christian polemics. We agree with Tom Smail, Andrew Walker and Nigel Wright, when they say:

> From the point of view of systematic theology, it could be said that theology has four tasks: eirenics, polemics, apologetics and dogmatics. Eirenical and polemical theology are disputes internal to Christian faith, and apologetics is the defence and promotion of Christianity to those outside the Church. While dogmatics is concerned with the explication and elucidation of orthodox doctrines, eirenics and polemics are more typically reserved for theological issues of great importance (*theologoumena*), but not necessarily dogmatic ones. Nevertheless, when dogmatic issues are at stake in the Church, we can properly say that polemical theology (often of an astringent nature) is necessary.[2]

It must be remembered that the great credal and confessional statements of the church arose out of polemical theology — they were hammered out on the anvil of controversy. We certainly are not claiming to be engaging in polemics on this grandiose scale; we are not claiming that dogmatic issues concerning the orthodox confession of faith are at stake when discussing the 'Toronto Blessing'. Nevertheless, we do believe that the issues at stake are of great hermeneutical and theological significance and, when this is the case, polemics is the traditional and appropriate Christian theological response. In addition, Mark Stibbe is a respected biblical scholar; he knows that within the scholarly community ideas are presented publicly in the form of papers

---

[2] Tom Smail, Andrew Walker and Nigel Wright, *Charismatic Renewal: The Search for a Theology*, pp. 171–2, n. 2.

and monographs. Once out in the public academic arena every scholar's work is subject to the examination and critique of fellow scholars. As a result of such examination some ideas may be modified as appropriate and others may be regarded as standing the test. This is the normal way in which scholarship is advanced in the academic community. Stibbe is a member of that community and, on publishing a book, can expect appropriate feedback from that community. Indeed Stibbe's academic credentials are highlighted in the brief biographical information at the beginning of his book. All the contributors to this volume are also members of the academic community, albeit junior ones! As such we regard it as part of our duty to respond where there are substantial disagreements.

However, and this is most important, we do not write primarily as academics. We write as people who are passionately concerned about the church (not that the two are mutually exclusive!). We regard ourselves as charismatics who are concerned to see genuine evidence of the life of the Spirit in the church and, as such, are critical of much of current charismatic praxis. We do not believe, for example, that the emphasis on power in much of the charismatic movement today, where it is devoid of an emphasis on the cross, is a mark of the Spirit at work.[3] Consequently, to be true to our own convictions, we feel it is important to engage in such polemics, following Paul's advice in 1 Thessalonians 5:19–21: 'Do not quench the Spirit. Do not despise prophecies, *but test everything*; hold fast to what is good . . .'

For Paul, being true to the Spirit and testing everything were not incompatible; on the contrary, being true to the Spirit necessitated testing everything. We want to stand firmly in this Pauline tradition.

Four Important Questions

Each of the following four papers is a discrete unit, engaging with some aspect of Mark Stibbe's book, which is a highly

[3] See the very important chapter by Tom Smail entitled 'The Cross and the Spirit' in *Charismatic Renewal, pp*. 49–70.

articulate defence of the 'Toronto Blessing'. It contains arguments with which anyone who has reservations about the movement will have to engage. We believe, however, that the papers do more than simply interact with Stibbe. Each of them addresses interpretational issues which we believe are of importance for all Christians.

In the first paper I take issue with Stibbe's chapter concerning the cultural reasons for the current phenomena associated with the 'Toronto Blessing.'[4] I am studying for a PhD in biblical studies at the University of Sheffield and, although I am not a professional sociologist, my area of interest lies in sociological approaches to the New Testament. The first part of the paper highlights some of the difficulties in Stibbe's argument that God uses ecstatic phenomena to attract an ecstatic culture. The second half argues that Stibbe fails to address sociological factors at work within the church which have predisposed some Christians to embrace the ecstatic phenomena of the 'Toronto Blessing'. After identifying some of those factors, the paper concludes that sociological analysis is needed to counter-balance the large claims that are being made of the Blessing. If an alternative sociological account is possible — and I believe it is — then, at the very least, it should serve as a caution to those who would claim that the phenomena are self-evidently manifestations of the Holy Spirit.

The second paper analyses the principle of interpretation which Stibbe calls 'Pentecostal' or 'This-is-That' hermeneutics. The author, Mark Smith, obtained his doctorate in biblical studies at the University of Sheffield. Arguing that, in the end, Stibbe's approach does not assign any significant authoritative role to Scripture, despite protestations to the contrary, he concludes that a 'This-is-That' approach inevitably results in reading one's own messages into the biblical text rather than letting the Bible speak its message.

The third paper is by Vivien Culver, who is a graduate in biblical studies from the University of Sheffield. She investigates Stibbe's analysis of the biblical references to laughter in the light of modern linguistic theory, concluding that his analysis is

---

[4] This paper is a revised and greatly expanded version of a paper entitled 'New Churches and the "Toronto Blessing" ' which was previously circulated at the Sheffield Consultation on the Toronto Blessing held on 25 November 1994.

fundamentally flawed and that he fails to construct a convincing biblically validated case for ecstatic laughter. She goes on to examine another approach, not taken by Stibbe, adopted by some who seek to authenticate the unusual phenomena associated with the 'Toronto Blessing' — namely that the phenomena should be regarded as 'non-biblical' rather than 'unbiblical'. Claims that the phenomena are responses to the very presence of the Holy Spirit himself surely necessitate much more evidence than merely that the Bible does not disapprove of the phenomena.

The paper by John Lyons[5] critiques Stibbe's use of the Gamaliel principle, providing an historical overview of the way this has been used to evaluate various movements in church history. He examines the text of Acts to see what Luke's purpose in narrating the Gamaliel incident in Acts 5 might have been. The work of the Dutch theologian C.G. Berkouwer is cited, suggesting that we can only say of God's workings in history what an holistic reading of the Scriptures allows us to say. Thus there are historical, textual, and theological reasons why the use of the Gamaliel principle should play no part in Christian theology, especially in any attempt to formulate a response to a new movement.

We hope that these papers may contribute to an open debate on the nature of the 'Toronto Blessing'. We do not, in any way, consider our contribution to be the last word on the subject. We recognize that by offering these contributions for consideration, we are inviting response and critique. We welcome this and trust that further constructive criticism, such as we hope ours has been, will aid the Christian community as we all strive to become more like the one who is himself the Truth.

Lloyd Pietersen

Bibliography

Smail, T., Walker, A., and Wright, N., *Charismatic Renewal: The Search for a Theology* (London: SPCK, 1995).

Stibbe, M., *Times of Refreshing: A Practical Theology of Revival for Today* (London: Marshall Pickering, 1995).

[5] John Lyons is currently studying for a PhD in biblical studies from the University of Sheffield. An earlier version of his paper on the Gamaliel principle was delivered at the Centre for the Bible and Theology in the University of Sheffield.

Chapter 1
Ecstatic Phenomena for an Ecstatic Culture?

It is often argued that the 'Toronto Blessing' is in some way linked to the way our society is today. God has permitted — or indeed directed — it because it corresponds in some way to our present condition and needs.

In chapter 3 of his book Stibbe uses this argument in a way which is interesting but, I believe, mistaken. He argues that in the West we are living in an 'ecstatic' or 'addictive' society. Such a society promotes a 'lifestyle of ecstatic, mood-altering and escapist activities'[1] which are invariably forms of addiction. This ecstatic nature of our society is most poignantly symbolized by the drug commonly known as 'Ecstasy'. Stibbe suggests that 'God always operates in a guise which is appropriate to the culture concerned.'[2] Consequently, God is currently working through the ecstatic phenomena associated with the 'Toronto Blessing' in order to attract the current generation, which is preoccupied with the search for transcendence through ecstatic experiences. Stibbe proposes 'charismatic intoxication' as the divine alternative to society's demand for other forms of addiction and cites Ephesians 5:15–20 in support of this. Finally, he argues that when revivals have occurred previously in addictive societies they have often involved a high degree of ecstatic phenomena. He illustrates this by indicating the addictive nature of eighteenth-century British society as the context in which the revival associated with the Wesleys and Whitefield occurred. Stibbe concludes his chapter with some helpful warnings

---

1 *Refreshing*, p. 72.
2 Ibid., p. 71.

concerning the dangers of focusing on the manifestations associated with the 'Toronto Blessing'.

It is not my purpose in this chapter to argue with Stibbe's description of Western culture as ecstatic and addictive. Such elements can certainly be discerned in our culture although, in my view, culture is too complex a phenomenon to be categorized in such a general fashion. I have two basic arguments with Stibbe's position. First, I am concerned about his use of the doctrine of the incarnation to support the argument that God is currently working through ecstatic phenomena to reach an addictive generation. Second, Stibbe's method is to provide a sociological analysis of society and then argue that the church must adapt itself to the ecstatic needs of society; what he manifestly fails to do is to analyse the sociological factors at work *in the church* which have predisposed the church to embrace such ecstatic phenomena. I will deal with the first of these concerns briefly and will devote the bulk of the chapter to a sociological account of the reasons why the 'Toronto Blessing' has been so readily accepted by many churches.

1. Cultural Engagement does not Imply Cultural Conformity

Stibbe makes much in his chapter of the fact that God always operates in a guise which is appropriate to the culture concerned. The truth of this statement depends on what is meant by 'appropriate'. On the one hand, Stibbe appears to equate appropriateness with comprehensibility. For example, he states:

> When God became a human being in Palestine, he did not choose to appear as a Scandinavian blond, as in so many Sunday School paintings. He became a Jewish boy who grew up into a thoroughly Jewish-looking young adult. That young man did not speak the language of Hollywood but the languages of first-century Palestine . . . Furthermore, when Jesus began his ministry, he conducted it in a way that was comprehensible to Palestinians of the time.[3]

[3] *Refreshing*, p. 72. Used with the permission of the Publishers, Harper Collins.

This is, of course, true. However, for the church to be culturally relevant or comprehensible does not imply that it should simply conform to the surrounding culture. For it is also manifestly true that the Jewish Jesus did not simply conform to his Jewish culture. His ministry was comprehensible to the culture but was also a profound challenge to it. Indeed, even this notion of comprehensibility has to be qualified. God worked powerfully through the ministry of both John the Baptist and Jesus yet both were, in some respects, incomprehensible to the generation that Jesus addressed: 'John came neither eating nor drinking, and they say, 'He has a demon'; the Son of Man came eating and drinking, and they say, 'Look, a glutton and a drunkard, a friend of tax collectors and sinners!' (Matt. 11:18–19).[4]

On the other hand, Stibbe seems to imply a very close relationship between appropriateness and cultural conformity:

> Since ours is a largely Dionysian culture — *a culture of addicts looking for ecstasy* — God has chosen to operate during this time of refreshing by permitting many ecstatic phenomena — such as shaking, fainting, falling over, weeping, laughing, roaring, and generally drunken behaviour. All of this looks to outsiders just like Dionysian abandonment. It feels to cynical observers like possession, inebriation, loss of control and so on. But in a Dionysian culture, God graciously respects the needs of the hour. Since one of the deep needs of many people is the need for ecstasy, the Lord allows us to experience the uninhibited joy of knowing Jesus Christ in a number of varied, ecstatic ways — including some which look very strange.[5]

In other words, to meet the needs of an addictive culture God provides an alternative form of addiction in the form of the phenomena of the 'Toronto Blessing'. Indeed Stibbe specifically speaks of 'charismatic intoxication' as the 'divine alternative'.[6] Here Stibbe is on dangerous ground. He implies that there is to be no critique of addiction as such; addiction still characterizes

---

4 All biblical quotations are from the NRSV unless otherwise indicated.

5 *Refreshing*, pp. 84–5; my italics.

6 Ibid., pp. 80–4.

the Christian community, only it is now charismatic addiction rather than ingestive, process, relational, ideological, or technological addiction.[7] Interestingly, Stibbe himself refuses to carry through the logic of his argument. He notes in his appendix that people are being encouraged to receive as much of the 'blessing' as possible and to keep coming back for more experiences of the 'blessing'. Such encouragement might seem highly appropriate if the 'Toronto Blessing' were indeed God's alternative form of intoxication. The whole point of addiction is that one keeps coming back for more! However, Stibbe is emphatic that such encouragement 'is very dubious teaching'. Indeed, he goes as far as saying that such 'selfish charismatic praxis will lead us perilously close to blaspheming against the Holy Spirit . . .'[8] At this point Stibbe appears to be profoundly self-contradictory: he criticizes the addictive nature of the movement when he has previously argued for it as an alternative form of addiction — God's provision for 'a culture of addicts looking for ecstasy'!

Stibbe does expect the church to provide a radical alternative to the culture;[9] however, it is difficult to see how ecstatic phenomena in the church provides a *radical* alternative to the quest for ecstasy in society. Stibbe looks to Ephesians 5:18–20 for support, rightly arguing that in this passage Christians are presented with three lifestyle choices in the form of a 'not . . . but' construction. These are:

> not unwise, but wise (v. 15)
> not foolish, but understanding (v. 17)
> not intoxicated by wine, but filled with the Spirit (v. 18)

Stibbe claims that, in the third of these choices, 'it is fairly certain that Paul is contrasting two forms of intoxication — one involving wine, the other involving the Holy Spirit.'[10] This completely ignores the fact that, in each of these choices, the second item of the pair is *contrasted* with the first. Wisdom is not a different form of being unwise; understanding is not a

[7] This is how Stibbe categorizes the various forms of addiction in Western culture; *Refreshing*, pp. 72–6.
[8] Ibid., p. 178.
[9] See, for example, *Refreshing*, p. 89.
[10] Ibid., p. 83.

different form of foolishness; similarly, *being filled with the Spirit is not a different form of intoxication*. Being filled with the Spirit is the divine alternative as Stibbe rightly acknowledges; but the Christian alternative to Dionysian inebriation[11] is surely not some sort of charismatic intoxication. In the Greek text the exhortation to be filled with the Spirit is followed by three participles which refer to the consequences of being filled with the Spirit. These are: singing (v. 19), giving thanks (v. 20), and mutual submission (v. 21). Stibbe, in fact, rightly comments that the Christian alternative to Dionysian inebriation is:

> an alternative in which they could worship with psalms, hymns and spiritual songs (as opposed to frenzied dancing); in which they could sing and make music in their hearts to the Lord (not to Dionysus); in which they could enjoy the true God-given order for domestic relationships (Eph. 5:22 — 6:4), rather than the wild disorder of the Dionysian cult.[12]

The suggestion that this divine alternative is a form of intoxication simply does not follow. It is much more likely that *intoxication* is being contrasted with *sobriety* as in 1 Thessalonians 5:6–8. One commentator notes that the verb *nēphō* (to be sober) in 1 Thessalonians 5:6,8 'is used in the NT only figuratively in the sense of being free from every form of mental *and spiritual "drunkenness"*, and thus it comes to mean "be well balanced, self-controlled" '.[13] According to Galatians 5:23 self-control is among the fruit of the Spirit.

---

[11] Stibbe accepts that Ephesians was written by Paul and addressed to the church in Ephesus. He follows the argument of C.L. Rogers, 'The Dionysian Background of Ephesians 5:18', *Biblica Sacra* 136 (1979), pp. 249–57, who suggests that the cult of Dionysus with its wild, drunken practices flourished in Ephesus at the time and provides the historical background to Ephesians 5:18. Whether the Dionysian cult is specifically in view here remains a matter of scholarly debate; see, for example, A.T. Lincoln, *Ephesians*, Word Biblical Commentary 42, pp. 343–4.

[12] *Refreshing*, p. 82.

[13] G.W. Knight III, *Commentary on the Pastoral Epistles*, 1992, p. 456. This is the view too of Louw & Nida; the electronic version of Louw & Nida's *Greek-English Lexicon of the New Testament Based on Semantic Domains* states: '*a*: (a figurative extension of meaning of *nēphō* "to be sober," in the sense of not being drunk,

Furthermore, apart from the contrast between drunkenness and sobriety in 1 Thessalonians 5:6–8, this interpretation also fails to take account of the situation at Corinth. In 1 Corinthians it appears that ecstatic phenomena were highly rated, leading to disorder in the worship services. In this context Paul argues for worship that is charismatic, but non-ecstatic, (1 Cor. 14). He places great emphasis on the use of the mind, on order, and on the control of prophecy and glossolalia. Paul does not endorse 'charismatic intoxication' at Corinth! In addition, it seems likely that, in 2 Corinthians, Paul is contending with other workers who are highly regarded by the Corinthian community because of their emphasis on miracles and ecstatic experiences. In 2 Corinthians 10–13 Paul seems to be fighting to defend his apostolic credentials. Ralph Martin, after a careful discussion concerning the identity of Paul's opponents in this section of 2 Corinthians, concludes:

> . . . 'another Jesus' for the opponents is the wonder–working Jesus, rather than Paul's crucified and risen Lord. The alien 'spirit' is the *spirit of power and ecstasy* which these messengers claimed to possess and embody in their ministry, rather than the Spirit of Christ which Paul exemplified. The new 'gospel' is the message of power and present glory, based on demonstrable tokens of the divine and evidences of authority in their lives as Christ's servants (v. 13), rather than Paul's kerygma of the suffering Christ whose power is displayed incognito and in patient love (13:3, 4).[14]

---

[13] *continued.* probably not occurring in the NT) to be in control of one's thought processes and thus not be in danger of irrational thinking — "to be sober-minded, to be well composed in mind" . . . *b*: to behave with restraint and moderation, thus not permitting excess — "to be self-controlled, to be restrained, to be moderate in one's behavior, to be sober" . . . It is possible that in 1 Thess. 5.8 *nēphō* means lack of drunkenness, but most scholars interpret the use of *nēphō* in the NT as applying to a broader range of soberness or sobriety, namely, restraint and moderation which avoids excess in passion, rashness, or confusion.'

[14] R.P. Martin, *2 Corinthians*, Word Biblical Commentary 40, p. 341; my italics. Used with the permission of Word Publishing.

Paul does not discount ecstatic experiences, but it is clear that his gospel does not seek to promote such experiences.[15] Paul does not propose ecstasy in the church as the answer to the needs of the ecstatic culture in Corinth.[16]

Furthermore, Stibbe's citation of the revival in eighteenth-century Britain is problematic for his position. He provides some impressive statistics showing the degree of alcohol addiction in the eighteenth-century, together with some horrific accounts of the violence of that age, and uses these to support the not unreasonable contention that eighteenth-century British society was also addictive or ecstatic. He notes the irrelevance of the Anglican Church in this context, and argues that God provided an answer to the needs of that society through the ministry of people such as the Wesleys and Whitefield. God's provision included 'demonstrations of the Spirit, with great power'.[17] However, the leaders of the revival do not appear to have regarded such demonstrations of the Spirit as an alternative form of ecstasy. Stibbe himself recognizes that a characteristic of the eighteenth-century revival was 'a lifestyle of holy abstinence'.[18] Taking this in conjunction with Ephesians 5:18–20, it appears the radical divine alternative to an addictive eighteenth-century society was not an alternative ecstatic experience, but a demonstrable lifestyle of self-control. It is difficult to see how Stibbe's concept of ' "decaffeinated discipleship" (a lifestyle with all addictive elements removed)'[19] is compatible with his notion of 'charismatic intoxication'.

It appears that Stibbe's use of the doctrine of the incarnation to argue that '*God operates in a guise which is appropriate to the culture*

---

[15] See 2 Corinthians 12:1–10.

[16] If Stibbe wants to argue for a Dionysian background to Ephesians 5:18 he has to contend with the possibility that the Dionysian cult was also affecting the church at Corinth. He notes that the cult was widespread in the ancient world. The Dionysian practice of women wearing their hair loose has, in fact, been proposed as the background for Paul's comments on head covering in 1 Corinthians 11:2–16.

[17] *Refreshing*, p. 91.

[18] Ibid., p. 92.

[19] Ibid., p. 93.

concerned'[20] comes dangerously close to advocating cultural conformity. We have seen that the historical Jesus both challenged his contemporary Jewish culture and was, in some ways, incomprehensible to it. A more appropriate use of incarnation language would encourage churches to engage the surrounding culture without being conformed to it.

2. Sociological Factors Affecting the Church

The argument that the phenomena of the 'Toronto Blessing' enable the church to engage with culture in relevant ways is decidedly one-sided. Stibbe fails to provide a sociological analysis of the church in the West in order to ascertain internal factors which have predisposed the church to embrace the 'Toronto Blessing'. One way of identifying such sociological clues is to focus on the so-called 'new churches'. I have been involved with such churches for the past 21 years, for much of that time in some leadership capacity, but the analysis presented here has broader relevance.[21] Although I do not pretend that it is either exhaustive[22] or sufficiently rigorous (since I am not a professional sociologist), nevertheless I believe that the factors outlined need to be taken into account here in evaluating Stibbe's analysis.

(1) Dissociative States

The phenomena associated with the 'Toronto Blessing' have brought the question of dissociative states into focus. Patrick Dixon acknowledges that the phenomena often occur as a result

[20] *Refreshing*, p. 72; Stibbe's italics.

[21] A number of 'new church' leaders are, in any case, highly influential in the broader charismatic scene in the UK.

[22] In particular I am conscious that I have not provided an analysis of power language in charismatic circles. I believe that such an analysis would prove highly significant both in view of the concept of 'power encounters' associated with John Wimber, and the widespread feeling of powerlessness in the face of secular society experienced by many charismatic Christians. However, such an analysis would probably require a monograph in its own right to do it justice.

of altered states of consciousness.[23] Mark Stibbe refers to them as 'ecstatic phenomena'.[24] Philip Richter notes: 'The Toronto Blessing stands out from ordinary religious experience in being predominantly ecstatic, and in some cases revelational, in form.'[25] I would suggest that the centrality of such ecstatic phenomena is something new as far as the charismatic movement, as distinct from the earlier Pentecostal movement, is concerned. Although ecstatic phenomena have always appeared at the margins of the movement, one of the hallmarks of the charismatic movement has been its emphasis on self-control. Glossolalia, prophecy, etc. have all been perceived as being under the control of the person exercising the gift. Paul's emphasis on order in the operation of the gifts of the Spirit, as found in 1 Corinthians 14, has always been central in charismatic exposition of spiritual gifts. This is far removed from the out-of-control character of dissociation. In fact, much of what I have personally seen bears striking resemblance to the dissociative states witnessed by sociologists studying glossolalia in ecstatic Pentecostal and Spiritualist groups. Unlike much charismatic glossolalia,[26] these documented accounts concern groups in which glossolalia occurs only when in a state of dissociation — an altered state of consciousness. Many people who have experienced the 'Toronto Blessing' speak of being in such a 'switched off' state.[27]

---

[23] P. Dixon, 'Signs of Revival?' in 'Prayer & Revival', *Alpha* magazine (December, 1994), p. 4. See especially, P. Dixon, *Signs of Revival: Detailed historical research throws light on today's move of God's Spirit*. Dixon makes detailed comments on altered states of consciousness (or ASCs as he calls them) in chapter five entitled 'Medical Perspectives on Manifestations' (pp. 233–79).

[24] *Refreshing*, p. 85.

[25] 'God is not a Gentleman!', p. 6.

[26] The extensive use of Goodman's analysis of glossolalia which follows does not mean that I equate her examples with the charismatic phenomenon of 'speaking in tongues'. As stated above, the emphasis on self-control in many charismatic circles has meant that speaking in tongues has not generally occurred, in my experience, in a state of dissociation from everyday reality. I am, however, comparing Goodman's analysis of glossolalia with the current phenomena occurring in the 'Toronto Blessing'.

[27] The following is typical of much that I have heard: 'Within a minute or so, suddenly my mind became so relaxed. The nearest I can think of to describe it was when I had sodium pentathol years ago when I had major surgery', *Renewal* (October, 1994), p. 13.

Sociological studies have indicated that groups can be taught both dissociation and glossolalia by a charismatic leader.[28] F.D. Goodman's work involved detailed analysis of tape recordings made by other researchers during the services of a number of different religious groups. These included the Streams of Power movement in St Vincent island; a mid-western tent revival in Columbus, Ohio; the Umbanda spiritualist cult in Brazil, and various mainline Protestant churches in Texas. She also carried out her own detailed participant observation, and recorded on tape and film dissociative states and glossolalia among a Spanish-speaking Pentecostal congregation in Mexico City and a Mayan-speaking branch of the same denomination in Yucatan. From her analysis Goodman cites a number of cases of evangelists going to a new congregation in which there had been little or no glossolalia and causing outbreaks of dissociative states and glossolalia. Such instances of dissociation and glossolalia are clearly taught, according to Goodman, because the utterances of the members of the congregation quickly become stereotyped and mirror that of the person who guided them into the experience. Goodman discovered that those she was investigating broke into glossolalia only when in a state of dissociation — that is when they had withdrawn into an inner space and dissociated themselves from everyday reality. In this dissociative state other phenomena frequently occurred, such as shaking, catatonic-like states, and both auditory and visual hallucinations. In fact, on one occasion, Goodman herself involuntarily went into a state of dissociation during which she had a powerful vision of light. Many people testified to feelings of peace, or even euphoria, at the conclusion of the dissociative state. Most concluded that the experience was a manifestation of the Holy Spirit. This interpretation of the phenomenon inevitably resulted in glossolalia being perceived as a matter of prestige for the members of the community who had exhibited it. Conversely, those who had been members for some time without displaying glossolalia might well be criticized as being too sinful to receive it.

P.F. Esler, commenting on Goodman's work, states:

---

[28] E.g. F.D. Goodman, *Speaking in Tongues: A Cross-Cultural Study of Glossolalia*, cited in P.F. Esler, *The First Christians in their Social Worlds*, pp. 40–3.

> One of the most remarkable of her observations is the phenomenon of spontaneous glossolalia which occurs without the person concerned ever having witnessed it before (70). She relates that on one occasion in Yucatan 'a boy wandered into the church and, upon seeing some *hermanos* (i.e. male members of the congregation) going into glossolalia, also dissociated and produced a vocalisation. He never came back to the church.' Given that glossolalia is usually seen as a manifestation of the Holy Spirit, its appearance in someone who may be a complete non-believer inevitably prompts some theological explanation to make sense of the occurrence.[29]

Some of the parallels between ecstatic glossolalia and the current phenomena of the 'Toronto Blessing' are striking. In particular the case of the boy in Yucatan is paralleled by the experience of the *Daily Telegraph* reporter Mick Brown.[30] Serious attention has therefore to be given to the possibility that what actually happens in 'Blessing meetings' is that the phenomena are naturally induced and can possibly be compared to stage hypnosis or religious trance-inducing rituals. The following sections explore some possible reasons why so many charismatics have been prepared to enter dissociative states.

(2) Charismatic Context

It is interesting to note that, by and large, the 'Toronto Blessing' has affected churches which have already been influenced by the charismatic movement. The acceptance of the label 'charismatic' implies an expectation of certain phenomena. Consequently, members of such churches are already socialized into accepting unusual phenomena in their worship gatherings. For example, much is usually made of 1 Corinthians 12:7, 'To each is given the *manifestation* of the Spirit for the common good.' Consequently,

---

[29] P.F. Esler, *op. cit.*, pp. 42–3 used with permission of the Publishers, Routledge; the number in brackets refers to the appropriate page in Goodman's book. The previous paragraph is taken from Esler's summary of Goodman's findings.

[30] See Mick Brown, 'Unzipper heaven, Lord, Ha-ha, ho-ho, he-he . . .', *Daily Telegraph Magazine* (Saturday, December 3, 1994), pp. 26–7, 28–30, and the article 'What happened next?', *Evangelicals Now* (February, 1995), pp. 1, 8.

manifestations have always been encouraged in charismatic circles; usually without a great deal of critical discernment. Here is one example: it has long been received wisdom in such circles that the practice of specifically identifying various needs within the congregation publicly, without previously being told what those needs are, is to be equated with the 'word of knowledge' of 1 Corinthians 12:8. The act of identifying the need is often considered as sufficient proof that something supernatural has occurred. In my experience these 'words of knowledge' often occur in a healing context—physical ailments are identified and those who respond subsequently receive prayer for healing. Often immediate testimony is encouraged. In the highly charged atmosphere the pressure to testify to healing can be enormous. The result is that the charismatic congregation hears an *oracle* (the 'word of knowledge') and perceives a *miracle* (the testimony to healing). What fails to happen all too often is any critical follow-up of the claims to healing. Consequently, 'miracles and oracles' frequently occur without any critical evaluation. Indeed, any such evaluation can even be perceived as an act of unbelief. Furthermore, these sorts of meetings are commonplace, at least in 'new church' circles. Consequently, charismatics are socialized into an environment which expects miracles and oracles, *and in which 'miracles' and 'oracles' are perceived regularly to occur*. This has been going on for many years in the charismatic movement and is very much part of the internal charismatic scene. This internal social context is, I believe, of prime significance for understanding the 'Toronto Blessing'. So is the persistence of this demand for miracles and oracles—what sociologists call thaumaturgical demand.

(3) Charismatic Demand for Newness

Many 'new churches' operate with a Spirit-tradition dualism. Tradition is perceived as a dirty word; spontaneity is perceived as a mark of the Spirit. For example, the motto of the 'new church' in which I was a leader for many years used to be: 'Constant change is here to stay!' In this context there is a continual demand for something new. There can be nothing 'ordinary' about Christianity; the Christian life must be seen to be extraordinary. This inevitably has an immensely destabilizing effect and has served to fuel thaumaturgical demand; such charismatics quickly become dissatisfied with the latest arrival on the charismatic scene and look for something which will give them even more charismatic 'buzz'. I believe this can easily be documented: itinerant healing and prophetic ministries; John Wimber's emphasis on 'power evangelism'; the emphasis on the demonic and 'spiritual warfare' popularized by Frank Perretti's novels; the 'Kansas City prophets'; and now the 'Toronto Blessing'. It is interesting that each emphasis centres on experience. It is also interesting to note how many times future mission has been promised as an apologetic for present introspection. The current emphasis on the 'Toronto Blessing' being a time of refreshing for God's people prior to mission has a well-worn ring to it; the promise has often been reiterated in the immediate past, but has repeatedly failed to deliver.

(4) The Institutionalization of Charisma

Paradoxically, despite the constant demand for something new, charismatic churches have become increasingly institutionalized in structure. This point is well made by Philip Richter.[31] As Weber noted, charismatic authority is inherently unstable and is transformed over time into bureaucratic or traditional authority. Richter rightly notes that, at least in the case of the 'new churches', in the early days the leaders exercised charismatic authority in the Weberian sense. However, with the growth of such churches and the extensive networking that has taken place, leadership style has been transformed into bureaucratic authority. Under the influence of growth and business management strategies leaders have become exhausted and close to burnout. In this context, Richter argues, the 'Toronto Blessing' has provided an opportunity for some leaders to have 'a kind of religious "mid-life crisis" in which they have radically re-evaluated the direction of their ministries'.[32] For leaders close to

[31] P.J. Richter, ' "God is not a Gentleman!": The Sociology of the Toronto Blessing', in S.E. Porter & P.J. Richter (eds.), *The Toronto Blessing — Or Is It?*, pp. 5–37 (especially, 22–4).

[32] 'God is not a Gentleman!', p. 23.

burnout the emphasis on refreshing[33] is most welcome.[34] Stibbe's honest self-description is highly relevant here, and probably speaks for many charismatic leaders:

> In July of 1994 I was desperate. My own spirituality was one of performance rather than reality. I was leading my church as if I was on fire for the Lord when in truth I was little more than a smouldering wick. More than that, I was standing up at conferences and speaking with a dynamism which owed far more to my flesh than to God's Spirit. I had become a prey to vanity and ambition, and as a consequence was tired, anxious, and depressed. Ministry had become a burden to me. The church where I serve full time was proving to be extremely stressful. Sleep had become a premium. All I could see was the cost of leadership. I had truly become weary in well-doing.[35]

Furthermore, Richter argues, the very adoption of modern business management styles leads in turn to the nostalgic desire for the return of a more charismatic style of leadership.

(5) The Routinization of 'New Church' Meetings

I would add one further comment to Richter's analysis. The emphasis on constant change, which I mentioned in the previous section, is, of course, impossible to sustain in the course of everyday life of the church. Some degree of routine is inevitable if church meetings are not to become anarchic. Paradoxically, therefore, whereas 'new churches' were continually looking for the new, their meetings became increasingly routinized over time. Despite the anti-traditional, anti-liturgical rhetoric, I believe that

---

[33] However, the attempt to ground this emphasis on refreshing biblically by an appeal to Acts 3:20 utterly fails to do justice to the context of that passage which concerns an appeal by Peter to non-Christian Jews to repent. See, for example, S.E. Porter, 'Shaking the Biblical Foundations?' in *The Toronto Blessing — Or Is It?*, pp. 38–65 (48–9).

[34] Ironically though, additional services are frequently laid on specifically for the purpose of 'Toronto Blessing' ministry. This has led to some of the very leaders whom I have heard espousing this concept of refreshing admitting that they are thoroughly exhausted by the sheer volume of ministry being generated.

[35] *Refreshing*, p. 139.

someone versed in 'new church' forms of worship could go to any 'new church' in Britain and have a pretty good idea as to what would happen in any given meeting. In other words, despite the rhetoric, a 'new church' liturgy has emerged. This, I suggest, produced a situation in which an increasing number of people in such churches had instinctively recognized this, could no longer identify with the current liturgy, and were crying out for a richer liturgy rooted in the orthodox tradition of the church. Certainly in some cases they voted with their feet! What the 'Toronto Blessing' has done, at least for 'new churches', has been to revitalize the meetings. Naturally, in the absence of a theology which adequately embraces tradition, 'new church' congregations will eventually seek something beyond the manifestations associated with the 'Toronto Blessing'.

On the other hand, the welcome emphasis in many 'new churches' on the relevance of the gospel to the whole of life, together with the routinization of meetings, has meant that increasingly meetings as such have not been perceived as the focal point of 'new church' life. This inevitably has led to some loss of status on the part of at least those leaders whose main role has been a public one in the context of meetings. What the 'Toronto Blessing' has done has been to restore the centrality of meetings to such churches. Leaders who have struggled with a sense of loss of status are back in demand as people flock to 'Blessing' meetings. I believe that this 'feel good' factor has been a subtle influence on the widespread endorsement of the 'Toronto Blessing' by 'new church' leaders.

(6) 'New Churches' and Thaumaturgy

There are additional sociological reasons why so many 'new churches' have embraced the phenomena of the 'Toronto Blessing'. I believe that if phenomena such as uncontrollable twitching, hysterical laughing, barking like dogs, and roaring like lions had occurred in the early days of such churches they would have been dismissed by the leaders as extreme religious behaviour. Members would not have been encouraged to engage in such practices.

The emphasis in the early days was on reality in the Christian life. Although some supernatural dimension to faith was, of course, accepted, 'supernaturalism' as such was strongly discouraged.[36] Gerald Coates's warning is typical:

> In certain circles there is a hidden law. All problems have to be resolved with a word from God, a tongue, a prophecy or a word of knowledge. If you have a sin problem you have got a demon. If you are insecure you were probably dropped out of your cot when you were 13½ days old and you need the healing of memories and so on. I am not belittling the manifestation of the spirit, *but I am coming to see that many Christians need some sane common-sense, not special 'spiritual' answers.*[37]

In the editorial of the same issue of *Fulness*, Graham Perrins wrote:

> When Jesus said 'I have come in order that you might have life — life in all its fulness', some have limited his meaning to include only spiritual life. Life then becomes synonymous with conventions, ministry, prayer meetings, the baptism in the Holy Spirit or some such experience.
>
> Nothing could be further from the truth. Life for Jesus could mean nothing less than a full-orbed experience of God's provision for the whole man. God intended that man should enjoy creation, that the whole of life should vibrate with his love, the common and the mundane throb with his glory, the small and insignificant fulfil his purpose.
>
> Some Christians are so intense in their spirituality that they cannot relax and enjoy God or his creation. They have an aura of religiosity that casts a shadow on the simple things of life.[38]

These quotations, from significant 'new church' leaders, demonstrate that they originally advocated a spirituality rooted in experiencing God in the context of ordinary, everyday life, which is markedly different from that associated with the 'Toronto Blessing'. In the latter, despite protestations to the

---

[36] I am using 'supernaturalism' to describe the belief that God usually engages with his creation in extraordinary, 'non-natural' ways.

[37] G. Coates, 'Being Yourself', *Fulness* 12 (undated), pp. 4–6 (6); my italics.

[38] G. Perrins, *Fulness* 12 (undated), p. 3.

contrary, the emphasis has been on finding God during ministry in 'Blessing' meetings. Early 'new church' spirituality was not meeting-oriented. The question, therefore, arises as to how a movement which began by relativizing the importance of meetings could become so caught up with an emphasis on personal ministry in the context of meetings.

(7) Millennialism, Cognitive Dissonance and Thaumaturgical Responses

Sociologically speaking, 'new churches' are best classified as 'conversionist' according to Bryan Wilson's sevenfold typology of new religious movements.[39] In other words the world is viewed as corrupt because human beings are corrupt. Transformation of the world can come about only through the transformation of human beings. However, human beings are incapable of bringing about their own transformation. This can be achieved only by supernatural means. Conversionist movements are 'not concerned simply with recruitment to a movement, but with the acquisition of a change of heart'.[40] However, there was also a strong millennialist[41] strand, at least in the early days of the 'new churches'.[42] Broadly speaking, it is my contention that the current emphasis on 'supernaturalism' in 'new churches' arises, in part at least, from the failure of previous millennial expectations. Many 'new churches' combined an emphasis on down-to-earth spirituality with a sense of eschatological imminence. Much of the rhetoric concerned the possibility of the church coming to full stature within one generation, with the consequent expectation of Christ's imminent return.[43] The following quotations are typical of this early 'new church' rhetoric:

---

[39] B.R. Wilson, *Magic and the Millennium: A Sociological Study of Religious Movements of Protest Among Tribal and Third-World Peoples*, pp. 18–30.

[40] Ibid., pp. 22–3.

[41] In the sense of the expectation of the imminent return of Christ.

[42] See, for example: A. Pullin, 'The Hope of His Calling', *Fulness* 13 (undated), pp. 22–3, and volumes 14 and 19 (undated) of *Fulness*.

[43] This was never conceived of as an 'any moment' return as in Dispensationalist teaching. Christ's return was seen as dependent upon the emergence of a mature church. Nevertheless, the belief that this could happen within one generation meant that there was a strong millenarian element to 'new churches'.

So we come to the momentous days in which we live. We are too well aware that the history of the Church has been one of ineffectiveness. It is equally certain that God must triumph and that he has committed himself to establishing his glory among his people, totally and irreversibly. The hour of victory is near. *We are witnessing the last great rise in the history of the people of God*. The prophetic voice is sounding again across the earth for those who will hear what the Spirit is saying to the churches.[44]

One of John's [in the Book of Revelation] most exciting *end-time predictions to this generation* concerns God's final harvest in the earth, to be gathered up in the last days. For these are to be days of unlimited spiritual outpouring. What has barely begun in this present charismatic visitation, will yet be climaxed *just ahead of us* in the greatest outpouring of the Holy Spirit ever seen upon the face of all the earth.[45]

Within weeks God began to write on my heart something of the true hope of the Church; the glorious hope of a bride made ready to meet her bridegroom; a city of transparency and beauty; a finished house for his eternal dwelling place; a redeemed and victorious people having returned to Zion, reflecting his glory and showing forth his praise; a highway of holiness on which the king would return, his enemies now his footstool, his people prepared to rule the earth with him. I saw that this age was not going to fade out, closed by the removal of the Church as an embarrassing failure, but that it was going to conclude in a blaze of glory; that the grace of God would triumph in bringing forth a generation of people who would be changed into the image of Jesus, waiting only for the final release of resurrection at the sound of the trumpet . . . God is arising now, his light is shining over the earth as the Holy Spirit speaks to the churches. A heart-cry is born in the people of God for the fulfilment of the eternal purpose, *the emergence*

[44] A. Pullin, 'The Sleeping Beauty', *Fulness* 14 (undated), p. 9; my italics.
[45] C. Schmitt, 'First Fruits', *Fulness* 19 (undated), p. 20; my italics.

of a company who will bring forth the fruits of the kingdom and come to the very stature of the Christ.[46]

'New church' teaching on the 'Ephesian 4 ministries' of apostle, prophet, evangelist, pastor and teacher, emphasized their eschatological role in bringing the church 'to the measure of the full stature of Christ' (Eph. 4:13).[47]

I think it is fair to say that, although there have been some significant changes on the church scene, many of the original 'new church' members expected far more to have happened twenty years further on than actually has. Millennial fervour has, to a large extent, dissipated. Sociologically, there are various well-documented responses to the turmoil which arises following the intense disappointment of millennial expectations. I know of a number of churches which have had to come to terms with profound disillusionment in recent years amongst their first generation members. This disillusionment can helpfully be examined sociologically and psychologically in terms of the notion of 'cognitive dissonance'.[48] By this I mean the profound sense of discrepancy between the hope that has been sustained and the actual course of events. 'Since there is often, although not always, a strong human compulsion to reduce such dissonance, the experience frequently produces a change of outlook.'[49] Often this change of outlook leads previously millenarian movements to adopt an introversionist response to the world by means of voluntary social, or even geographical, withdrawal.[50] In the case of 'new churches', however, I suggest that the response has been primarily a thaumaturgical one.

Bryan R. Wilson defines the thaumaturgical response as essentially concerned with supernatural relief from the individual's

---

[46] A. Pullin, 'The Hope of His Calling', pp. 22–3.

[47] I should know — this has been an emphasis in my own teaching ministry for years!

[48] I am using this term in a more general sense than that used in Festinger's somewhat discredited model found in L. Festinger, et al, *When Prophecy Fails: A Social and Psychological Study of a Modern Group that Predicted the Destruction of the World.*

[49] P.F. Esler, *op. cit.*, p. 99.

[50] See, for example, P.F. Esler, op. cit., pp. 110–30.

present and specific ills.[51] This response focuses on personal healing and blessing by supernatural means. 'Miracles and oracles, rather than the comprehension of new principles about life, are the instruments of salvation in this case.'[52] It seems to me, as stated above, that 'new churches' have become increasingly concerned with 'miracles and oracles'. In other words, the thaumaturgical element (which has always been a legitimate part of orthodox Christianity) is becoming more and more dominant. Wilson documents how, in third-world contexts, the thaumaturgical response actually thrives among 'conversionist' sects. I suggested above that 'new churches' are probably best classified, according to Wilson's typology, as 'conversionist'.

> The conversionist model . . . provides, in the emotional freedom on which conversionism relies, a context suitable for wonder-working and the distribution of special, particularized benisons. Local discretion is often sufficient to allow considerable latitude in the interpretation of basic teachings, and doctrine is never a supreme concern of conversionist movements. *The emphasis on a heart-experience can readily accommodate the direct operation of the deity in offering miracles, even if these contravene the specific expectations which a conversionist movement — at its most doctrinally pure — would acknowledge as legitimate.* The amalgamation of conversionist orientations and the demand for wonders, healings, and reassurance, is perhaps the most effective pattern of regulation for thaumaturgy.[53]

Furthermore, Wilson also notes that part of millennarian hope is inevitably concerned with thaumaturgical preoccupations. In the new age there will be no more death, sickness, etc. Consequently, when millennialism fades, one response is to seek to make these future elements much more immediately accessible. Thus millennarian movements are often transformed into thaumaturgical ones.[54]

51 *Magic and the Millennium*, pp. 24–5.
52 Ibid., p. 25.
53 Ibid., p. 131; my italics.
54 Ibid., pp. 348–83.

Wilson's analysis appears highly relevant to the question of the general 'new church' response to the 'Toronto Blessing'. 'New churches', as conversionist in orientation, have increasingly provided the environment in which thaumaturgical responses have flourished. This can easily be documented, as stated above. The last fifteen years or so have witnessed an emphasis on 'power evangelism', a strong emphasis on the demonic (both in terms of individual demonization and so-called 'spiritual warfare' against 'demonic' principalities and powers), an emphasis on personal prophecy and words of knowledge (particularly as exemplified by the 'Kansas City Prophets'), and now the 'Toronto Blessing'. This has led to an increasing elevation of experience over doctrine. Furthermore, as Wilson has shown, an increased thaumaturgical response is likely in situations where millennial hope has been disappointed. The fact that early hopes for the church have not materialized can easily explain the (subconscious) shift towards an emphasis on supernatural experience.

(8) Emotional Religion as the Triumph of Secularization

There has been much recent debate amongst sociologists of religion concerning the process of secularization. A number of sociologists see the resurgence of the emotional dimension in religion, of which the charismatic movement is a prime example, as evidence of a broader process of desecularization in society. The growth of present-day emotional renewals is associated with the failure of modernity to fulfil its promise of unlimited progress. As a result, some argue, the concept of secularization should either be dropped or completely revised. The French sociologist Danièle Hervieu-Léger, who has done extensive research on the charismatic movement, argues, on the other hand, that this view is too simplistic. In a stimulating and provocative article she suggests that emotional renewals are characterized by a tension between secularizing and desecularizing tendencies in the wider society, operating simultaneously. In this light it is possible to argue that the resurgence of emotional religion does not signify the end of secularization, but rather its triumph.[55]

Hervieu-Léger defines emotional religious communities as those in which there is an intensification of the expressive dimension primarily in terms of 'bodily involvement in prayer . . . the physical manifestation of community nearness, and the emotional intensity of intermember relationships through kissing, embracing, holding hands or shoulders, and so on'.[56] She consciously draws the definition wider than those groups in which the expressive dimension is particularly effervescent, although her analysis includes such groups. She notes that, alongside the importance of the body and the senses in emotional religion, there is also a mistrust of any kind of doctrinal or theological formulations. Emotional religion tends to be anti-intellectual. What is surprising, therefore, is that emotional religion in the West attracts so many members of the intellectual middle classes. This demands an explanation.

Hervieu-Léger builds on the work of sociologists such as W.J. Samarin who have analysed glossolalia and have concluded that such phenomena constitute a form of socio- religious protest. However, unlike the case of historical Pentecostalism, particularly in black communities, present-day emotional religion cannot be explained as protest against effective deprivation of all forms of expression. Instead, as exemplified by its ability to attract the intellectual middle classes, emotional religion 'reflects the social and cultural protest of those who master, because of their social origin, the symbols and references of the dominant culture'.[57] Thus, Hervieu-Léger argues, emotional religion must be seen partly as a protest by the intellectual middle classes against the success of their own secularization. As the great religious traditions are deprived of social and cultural relevance through the advance of secularization one appropriate response is the return of ecstasy. She suggests that

[55] Danièle Hervieu-Léger, 'Present-Day Emotional Renewals: The End of Secularization or the End of Religion?', in William H. Swatos, Jr. (ed.), *A Future for Religion: New Paradigms for Social Analysis*, pp. 129–48 (published in 1993 and reprinted by permission of the Publishers, Sage, London).

[56] Ibid., p. 133.

[57] Ibid., pp. 143–4.

'these "returns of ecstasy" might correspond to an impoverishment of the religious imagination in the form of a regressive desire for immediate contact with the supernatural, a reversion to the meager [*sic*] universe of orgy and magic.'[58] For Hervieu-Léger, the popularity of emotional religion amongst the intellectual middle classes is due to their almost complete assimilation into the secularization process. In this context there can be no recourse to traditional religious language.

> The purely emotional orientation of these people's religious quest for sense might thus be seen as the result of the very success of their assimilation into the universe of modern rationality — a success so total that it destroys the plausibility, even for themselves, of the traditional language used to express their religious experience. The only solution is to use an inarticulate language whose capacity for communication is essentially expressive and poetic — a metalanguage that, by definition, avoids direct confrontation with the language of modernity, from which traditional religious language emerged and proved unacceptable.[59]

Philip Richter cites Hervieu-Léger approvingly and concludes:

> The world of 'information superhighways' seems a million miles from the world of faith. If intellectual middle-class Evangelicals are finding that the Gospel does not seem to be 'speaking the same language' any more, one solution is to adopt the inarticulate meta-language of glossolalia, another is to embrace the non-verbal Toronto Blessing. Both solutions avoid head-on engagement with the language of modernity. In this way the Blessing can be seen as helping to mediate the acute contradiction between their religious 'cultural capital' and the day-to-day realities of living and working in the 1990s.[60]

If Hervieu-Léger is right then inarticulate phenomena such as those associated with the 'Toronto Blessing' indicate that the

---

[58] Ibid., p. 141.

[59] Ibid., p. 144.

[60] '"God is not a Gentleman!": The Sociology of the Toronto Blessing', in S.E. Porter and P.J. Richter (eds.), *The Toronto Blessing – Or Is It?* (London: Darton, Longman and Todd, 1995); used by permission of the Publisher, p. 34.

church is in a state of deep cultural captivity to the secularization process. Brian Walsh certainly believes this to be the case. He argues that the Western church has suffered the 'spiritual catastrophe' of enculturation.

> As a community of believers and as individuals we have, mostly against our best intentions, been thoroughly sucked in to our secular culture. This is what I mean by the term 'enculturation'. Our consciousness, our imagination, our vision has been captured by idolatrous perceptions and ways of life. The dominant worldview, the all-pervasive secular consciousness, has captured our lives.[61]

The analyses of scholars such as Hervieu-Léger, Walsh, and also Walter Brueggemann,[62] provide impressive counter-arguments against those who would wish to argue that phenomena such as the 'Toronto Blessing' indicate the demise of secularization. Furthermore, their analyses, if accepted, are deeply shocking; for they indicate that phenomena such as the 'Toronto Blessing', far from heralding a great spiritual revival, are actually symptomatic of the profound cultural captivity of the church. In this context what is needed is true 'prophetic imagination'. As Brueggemann states: 'The task of prophetic ministry is to nurture, nourish, and evoke a consciousness and perception alternative to the consciousness and perception of the dominant culture around us.'[63]

3. Conclusion

I have sought to show in the first part of this chapter that there are serious difficulties with Stibbe's proposal that charismatic intoxication is the divine alternative to society's demand for other forms of addiction. In the rest of this chapter I have argued that Stibbe's analysis of contemporary Western culture as ecstatic is one-sided;

---

[61] Brian J. Walsh, *Subversive Christianity: Imaging God in a Dangerous Time*, p. 29. The entire book is a passionate plea for a spiritually renewed imagination which serves to subvert the values of the dominant secular ideology within the Christian community.

[62] See Walter Brueggemann, *The Prophetic Imagination*.

[63] *Prophetic Imagination*, p. 13.

he fails to take account of sociological factors at work within the charismatic movement which have predisposed charismatic churches to embrace the ecstatic phenomena associated with the 'Toronto Blessing'. Many supporters of the 'Toronto Blessing' will object to any sociological analysis as inevitably reductionist as it brackets out any possibility of transcendental causal factors. However, the major claims that are being made for the 'Toronto Blessing' mean that such sociological analyses are especially required at the present time. If it can be argued sociologically that emotional religion such as the 'Toronto Blessing' is an indication of the cultural captivity of the church to the secularization process, and if it can be demonstrated sociologically that the current movement may be no more than a mass exploration of dissociation — a state which can be both learned and naturally induced — then this should at least give those who claim that these are 'manifestations of the Holy Spirit' pause for thought.

Bibliography

Brown, Mick, 'Unzipper heaven, Lord, Ha-ha, ho-ho, he-he . . .', *Daily Telegraph Magazine* (Saturday, December 3, 1994), pp. 26–7, 28–30

—, 'What happened next?', *Evangelicals Now* (February, 1995)

Brueggemann, W., *The Prophetic Imagination* (Philadelphia: Fortress, 1978)

Coates, G., 'Being Yourself', *Fulness* 12 (undated)

Dixon, P., 'Signs of Revival?' in 'Prayer & Revival', *Alpha* magazine (December, 1994)

Dixon, P., *Signs of Revival: Detailed historical research throws light on today's move of God's Spirit* (Eastbourne: Kingsway, 1994)

Esler, P.F., *The First Christians in their Social Worlds* (London: Routledge, 1994)

Festinger, L., et al, *When Prophecy Fails: A Social and Psychological Study of a Modern Group that Predicted the Destruction of the World* (New York: Harper & Row, 1964)

Goodman, F.D., *Speaking in Tongues: A Cross-Cultural Study of Glossolalia* (Chicago: University of Chicago Press, 1972)

Hervieu-Léger, Danièle, 'Present-Day Emotional Renewals: The End of Secularization or the End of Religion?', in William H.

Swatos, Jr. (ed.), *A Future for Religion: New Paradigms for Social Analysis* (London: Sage, 1993), 129–148

Knight III, G.W., *Commentary on the Pastoral Epistles* (Grand Rapids: Eerdmans / Carlisle: Paternoster, 1992)

Lincoln, A.T., *Ephesians*, Word Biblical Commentary 42 (Dallas: Word, 1990)

Louw & Nida, *Greek-English Lexicon of the New Testament Based on Semantic Domains*

Martin, R.P., *2 Corinthians*, Word Biblical Commentary 40 (Dallas / Milton Keynes: Word, 1986)

Perrins, G., *Fulness* 12 (undated)

Porter, S.E., 'Shaking the Biblical Foundations?' in *The Toronto Blessing – Or Is It?* (London: Darton, Longman & Todd, 1995), pp. 38–65

Pullin, A., 'The Sleeping Beauty', *Fulness* 14 (undated)

Richter, P.J., ' "God is not a Gentleman!": The Sociology of the Toronto Blessing', in S.E. Porter & P.J. Richter (eds.), *The Toronto Blessing – Or Is It?* (London: Darton, Longman & Todd, 1995), 5–37

Rogers, C.L., 'The Dionysian Background of Ephesians 5:18', *Biblica Sacra* 136 (1979), pp. 249–57

Stibbe, M., *Times of Refreshing: A Practical Theology of Revival for Today* (London: Marshall Pickering, 1995)

Walsh, B.J., *Subversive Christianity: Imaging God in a Dangerous Time* (Bristol: Regius Press, 1992)

Wilson, B.R., *Magic and the Millennium: A Sociological Study of Religious Movements of Protest Among Tribal and Third-World Peoples* (London: Heinemann, 1973)

Chapter 2

'This-is-That' Hermeneutics

One important, although comparatively unsensational, aspect of the 'Toronto Blessing' is the suggestion that it may lead Christians to read the Bible in a new way. A fairly straightforward example of this would be to try to find in the Bible examples of the strange physical phenomena associated with the 'Blessing'. I have written elsewhere about the problems raised by this approach.[1]

Other people (usually more skilled in biblical interpretation) would argue that the 'new way' of reading the Bible is more far-reaching. Mark Stibbe's book contains a good specimen of this method of interpretation, which he calls the 'This-is-That' approach — a title based on Peter's words in Acts 2:16 (KJV). The passage expounded is Ezekiel 47. I shall begin by examining his interpretation but we shall find that it raises a number of important questions about the way in which Bible texts may be applied to the present day.

1. Ezekiel 47

Ezekiel 47 contains a vision of a river flowing out from Israel's temple. As the river leaves the temple, it is described in four stages. In the first stage, nearest to the temple, the water is ankle-deep. As it flows further it becomes knee-deep, then waist deep, until finally it is too deep for one to touch the bottom. Stibbe says: 'I would like to propose . . . the following thesis: that in the twentieth century, we can speak of four main movements of God's Holy Spirit, and that these four 'waves' represent a

---

[1] See my book, *Testing the Fire.*

THIS which corresponds to the THAT which we find in Ezekiel 47:1–12.'[2]

The first wave in the twentieth century, he says, was the emergence of Pentecostalism in 1906. Then came the Charismatic Renewal in the 1960s, then what he calls the 'Protestant Evangelical Renewal' in the 1980s sparked by John Wimber and a fourth wave is coming, of which 'the Toronto phenomenon is the first sign'.[3] Stibbe believes that these four waves correspond to the pattern of four stages of the river in Ezekiel 47.

Stibbe acknowledges that 'there are obviously a couple of large claims within this thesis'.[4] First, that there have indeed been three waves of the Spirit this century and that there is a fourth coming. He considers this claim 'to be historically sound'.[5] Since I am not a church historian, and since my purpose is to discuss hermeneutics, I am content to leave on one side the merits of that claim, and to examine only the second 'large claim'. This is the claim that what we have seen in the twentieth century is the 'That' of Ezekiel 47. Stibbe admits it 'is a claim which is much harder [sc. than the historical claim about four waves] to sustain on academic and intellectual grounds'. However, he does not think that is too important because, 'In matters such as these we enter the realm of the prophetic, and academic scholarship has a poor track record when it comes to understanding and uttering prophecy.'[6]

At this stage, we need to ask a couple of important questions. First, what is meant by 'the realm of the prophetic'? And secondly, on what grounds is the claim thought to be sustained?

First then, in referring to 'the realm of the prophetic', does Stibbe mean that when we try to interpret Ezekiel 47 we are interpreting a prophetic book, and academic scholarship has usually offered rather poor treatments of such books? Or, alternatively, does he mean that the particular interpretation he is offering is prophetic, and academic scholarship is bad at dealing with such interpretations? There may be an element of the

[2] *Refreshing*, p. 10.
[3] Ibid., p. 10.
[4] Ibid., p. 10.
[5] Ibid., p. 10.
[6] Ibid., p. 10.

former in what he is saying (though he does not make it very clear), but it seems that the latter predominates in his thinking. Stibbe considers himself as being 'prophetic' in his *interpretation* of Ezekiel 47. Thus he speaks of the 'THIS-IS-THAT' approach to the Bible coming out of 'a prophetic sense' which comes to the 'Spirit-filled interpreter'.[7] And in support of his interpretation he notes the remarkable 'coincidence' that, a few weeks before he preached a sermon based on his interpretation, somebody else had preached at the same church a very similar sermon based on Ezekiel 47. A number of people had come up to him after the sermon and told him this, and then asked, 'What's going on?!' To which I replied, 'What's going on is that two people may be hearing similar things from the Lord.'[8]

This is the answer to our first question, concerning what is meant by 'the realm of the prophetic'. Stibbe means he is offering a prophetic interpretation given him by the Holy Spirit. We are also led to a provisional answer to our second question, 'On what grounds does Stibbe think his claim can be sustained?' He thinks the claim that the 'this' of what is going on now is the 'that' of Ezekiel 47, can be sustained on the grounds that *God gave him this interpretation*. This leads to the conclusion that its status, therefore, is the same as that which is given to the prophecies offered by charismatic and Pentecostal Christians all over the world. Accordingly, he advised his post-sermon questioners, 'What you need to do is to test and see.'[9]

At this stage, we can say that, in order to be hermeneutically consistent, this 'prophetic interpretation' of Ezekiel 47 should not be offered by proponents of the 'Toronto Blessing' as proof that the *Bible* prophesies the 'Blessing' or teaches that it is of God. It is the people who offer the interpretation, such as Stibbe, who are speaking (as they believe) prophetically. They are making use of words and pictures taken from the Bible as a part of their own prophecies, but it is not the Bible which is speaking. This, of course, goes on in countless churches all over the world all the time. There is nothing wrong with it in and of itself. Many excellent, truly edifying prophecies have been

---

[7] *Refreshing*, p. 7.
[8] Ibid., pp. 6–7.
[9] Ibid., p. 7.

given which use biblical language and imagery. (Although, of course, it is wrong if somebody claims that the use of such language proves the content of the prophecy is biblical and of God. Many terrible prophecies have been given which are expressed in biblical language but which are not inspired by the Spirit.) And it is right to say that such prophecies must be tested. Classically, Pentecostals and charismatics have argued that in doing this, the hearers must consider whether prophecies are 'biblical'. That is, their content must be in accord with biblical principles.

However, there is a problem. Stibbe is not content to claim merely that he has offered a prophecy which makes use of biblical imagery and language. Instead, he seems to say that, although his interpretation originally came to him by inspiration of the Spirit, now that it has come to him, what is going on in the 'Blessing' does actually correspond to what is spoken of in the text. There is a pattern, he thinks, set out in Ezekiel 47, which is being repeated in this century. It is a pattern of the way the Holy Spirit works in renewal. He admits that the Spirit does not have to stick to this pattern, for 'the ways of the Spirit are mysterious; they are like the desert wind in ancient Palestine (John 3:8)'. But then he says: 'At the very least, we can speak of a pattern of renewal portrayed in the Ezekiel text, a pattern involving four mighty and miraculous effusions of the Spirit from the heart of the Divine Presence. That . . . is a symbolic picture of what I believe has been happening (and indeed *is* happening) in the twentieth-century'.[10]

At this point Stibbe appears not simply to be offering a prophecy in which he uses the text but to be making the much stronger claim that the text itself teaches something, namely a pattern for renewal. He is also claiming the 'Toronto Blessing' fits into this pattern. Thus he is making the strong claim that in this way the 'Blessing' is biblical. Hermeneutically speaking, he has shifted from claiming to be prophesying to claiming biblical authority for what he is saying.

This means that we need to ask whether the text he appeals to does indeed fit his interpretation. *Does Ezekiel 47 offer a fourfold pattern for renewal?*

---

[10] *Refreshing*, pp. 10–11.

Ironically enough, though he fails to realize it, Stibbe's own exegesis of Ezekiel 47 shows it does not have a fourfold pattern of renewal. He says that when he first studied Ezekiel 47 three years ago and was struck by his sense of 'this' is 'that'. 'It was the number four which attracted my attention. Ezekiel has a fondness for that particular number: it occurs 40 times in the book. As early as Ezekiel 1:5 we are introduced to four living creatures. There are four main visions of Ezekiel as a whole. Four seems to be a key number. Why?'

His answer is significant. Why is four a key number? 'Because in Ezekiel's time it was a number *which symbolized totality or completeness*. Hence Ezekiel 37:9: 'Come from the four winds, O breath!' i.e. come from every corner of the earth'.[11]

This is absolutely correct. The number four does symbolize totality or completeness. But this fact ruins Stibbe's argument. The vision of the river in Ezekiel 47 is not intended to symbolize *four literal stages* of renewal. Stibbe pushes the details of the vision too far. Just as the four winds of Ezekiel 37:9 do not symbolize the breath of God coming in four stages, but rather coming *from everywhere*, so, the four depths (not waves, by the way!) of the river symbolize that *complete* renewal will come. It is 'over-interpretation' (reading too much out of the text) to claim anything more. The completeness is emphasized by the fact that when the river of Ezekiel 47 reaches its fourth stage, it is a river through which Ezekiel cannot pass (v. 5) and everywhere it goes it brings life.

It thus seems faintly ridiculous to claim that the text sets out a pattern for *the way* things will *actually* happen. The text promises *complete* renewal, and it *symbolizes* this by the number four. It does not promise four actual stages to renewal. Claiming that it does is like claiming that there really are four winds or four corners of the earth. In fact, it is the same kind of mistake made by Jehovah's Witnesses with the 144,000 of Revelatian 7:4. This number is symbolic of the enormous number of people saved by God and sealed safe from his wrath. But Jehovah's Witnesses have taken the number literally, thinking that only 144,000 people will finally attain everlasting life (though the fact that there

---

11 *Refreshing*, p. 9 (my italics).

are now more than 144,000 Jehovah's Witnesses has caused them to begin modifying this claim).

Having considered this specific example of 'This-is-that' hermeneutics, we are in place now to look at the general principles underlying it. Before showing why they are unacceptable we shall examine them.

2. This-is-That

Stibbe thinks that conventional types of Bible interpretation are not adequate for what he calls 'Pentecostal spirituality'[12] (in which he includes charismatic spirituality). He explains why: 'The primary task of exegesis involves us perceiving what the Father is doing right now amongst us . . . and then allowing the Holy Spirit to lead us to Bible texts which elucidate that work.'[13]

In contrast to more conventional exegesis, therefore, which moves from the text to the reader, Stibbe suggests that we should move from ourselves (our experience) to the text. When we do that, we will see (with the help of the Spirit) that our experience is, in a sense, already there in the text. Thus the text will, in some way, 'illuminate' our experience. As we have seen, this is what he calls a 'This-is-that' approach to Scripture.

There are three key elements to the 'This-is-that' approach:

1. We perceive what God is doing now.
2. We go to Bible texts which elucidate this.
3. By a kind of 'feedback loop', we allow the Bible texts to illuminate what is happening.

In some ways this scheme sounds very much like conventional Christian interpretation. For example, when a person becomes a Christian, they perceive that God is doing something in them (step 1). With the help of other Christians, they will go to Scriptures (step 2) that will help them understand what it means to become a Christian and help them live a Christian life (step 3). Similar processes are followed with the ongoing Christian life and with the life of the church.

[12] *Refreshing*, p. 4.
[13] Ibid., p. 5.

But there are important differences too. First, by 'what God is doing now', Stibbe means, not such things as conversion and other 'ordinary' spiritual matters, but *'extraordinary' matters*, such as the 'Toronto Blessing', understood as a world-changing, history-making event. Once we have judged (presumably by some sort of spiritual discernment[14]) that such extraordinary events are of God, he thinks it is possible to 'find' them in some sense predicted in the Bible. In asking the hermeneutical question, we are asking whether Stibbe's method of finding them in the Bible is acceptable.

This leads us to the second difference from 'conventional' interpretation. In the 'conventional' kind of interpretation which most Christians practise, the Bible is read according to what I am going to call the *original sense*. I will explain what this is in a moment. For the moment it is sufficient to say that, read according to the original sense, the Bible does not talk about the 'Toronto Blessing'; and so Stibbe offers a way of reading that is different from the way we normally read the Bible.

The third difference has to do with the *role of the Holy Spirit* in this reading process. Most Christians believe the Holy Spirit helps them understand the Bible in some way. But Stibbe makes it clear that with 'This-is-that' interpretation, the Holy Spirit takes a more active role than many would expect. With the 'This-is-that' approach, we allow the 'Holy Spirit to lead us to Bible texts'.[15] And, most importantly, the resulting interpretation is not subject to the usual tests we apply to Bible interpretations, such as, does it make proper sense of the words of the text? does it take account of the context? does it fit the genre? Instead, the interpretation is to be treated on a seemingly more 'spiritual' level. It is 'prophetic'. In particular, if it is 'a true work of the Spirit', then, 'One of the most important tests is whether the same interpretation is offered by other people who have had no contact with each other.'[16] Or again, 'One of the key questions to ask when looking at a prophetic interpretation . . . is, "Is the

---

[14] I have discussed the question of how we are to 'discern' what is going on in the 'Toronto Blessing' in *Testing Toronto*.

[15] *Refreshing*, p. 5.

[16] Ibid., p. 6.

same thing being said by others?" '[17] We shall return later to the question of whether this is a good means of testing.

Stibbe's view of the involvement of the Spirit is crucial. For it appears to imply that considerable status be assigned to such interpretations. They are of the nature of, 'God says . . .' It follows, presumably, that conclusions reached from such interpretations are of a highly authoritative nature. They appear to be reached in the name of both Scripture and the Holy Spirit. For example, by his interpretation of Ezekiel 47, Stibbe is saying in the name of Scripture and the Spirit that the 'Toronto Blessing' is truly a move of the Spirit following a pattern of renewal laid out in the Bible.

Because 'This-is-that' interpretation is claiming such a high status, it is important to ask whether it is based on an acceptable hermeneutic. Of course, if it is not claiming such a high status, we need not worry so much. But neither, in that case, need we take its conclusions too seriously!

(1) The Original Sense

Every discussion needs to have some agreed starting points. When two or more parties are considering a matter on which they wish to reach some agreement, they will succeed only if each party has something in common with the others. I am going to begin with the assumption that my readers share with me the belief that the Christianity they practise should be *biblical*.

Exactly what this word means in practice will vary to some degree. For some, the concept 'biblical' means that modern Christians should follow exactly the morality and practices laid out in the Bible (including some of the more 'difficult' parts of the Old Testament). For others, it means we should seek to live in a way that reflects the radical lifestyle of Jesus (but, not, for example, the lifestyle of biblical times, which tended to oppress women). These are just two possibilities of what the concept 'biblical' might be understood to mean by Christians. Without denying the complexity of this situation, I am going to assume that for all of us one defining characteristic of the concept

---

17 *Refreshing*, p. 6.

'biblical' has been, at least until recently, that the *original sense* of the biblical text is paramount.

By the 'original sense', I am indicating the meaning which the author of the text originally intended. Most of my readers, and most people involved in the 'Toronto Blessing', will agree that the original sense of the text is the one with which we have to deal. Thus in applying 1 Corinthians 14:35 ('the women should keep silence in the churches') the first group I mentioned a moment ago may, in seeking to be biblical, read and not allow any women to teach, preach, pray or prophesy in their church services. The second group, also seeking to be biblical, may argue that this text ought not to be applied in the modern situation. However, both groups will accept that it is the original sense of the text with which they must deal. The first group will say that the original sense was that the women in the earliest churches had to 'keep silence' and will argue that that must also be true in today's churches, while the second group will agree about the original sense but will argue that it need not be applied now.

In other words, for the vast majority of those who seek to be 'biblical' Christians, the original sense is of paramount importance, though there is considerable debate about how the original sense should be applied. Indeed, this is also true of Christians who do not choose to designate themselves as 'biblical'. The majority of Christians throughout the world hold the Bible in very high esteem, and most would say, at least in theory, that it is the Bible read according to its original sense which they seek to apply (admittedly in very different ways) to their lives.

It is possible to be a little more precise about the significance of the classical distinction between 'what the text meant' and 'what the text means'. Most people recognize that what a Bible text says to us today is not precisely the same as what it said to its original readers. An obvious example is Philippians 4:2–3a, where Paul says, 'I entreat Euodia and I entreat Syntyche to agree in the Lord. And I ask you also, true yokefellow, help these women.' For the Philippian Christians, these words meant that they should help two important members of their church, Euodia and Syntyche, to overcome their dispute. But most would agree that for modern readers, the meaning is somewhat different: wherever there are disputes among us, we should seek to help those who are disputing to be reconciled. The two meanings are related but not the same.

It seems reasonable to say that what the text means is different from, but constrained by, what the text meant originally. The phrase 'constrained by' is very important. The text cannot mean *anything*. Paul's words, for example, cannot be said to mean that we should antagonize each other, causing disputes to arise and continue among us. If we claimed that that is what Philippians 4:2–3a means today, we would not be constrained by the original meaning, the original sense. Indeed we would be offering an interpretation which goes against the original sense.

This is not to say that discovering the original sense is always easy. It is very difficult to be completely sure about the original meaning of some biblical texts. An extreme example is found in 1 Corinthians 15:29, where Paul refers to the practice of being baptized on behalf of the dead. The problem is that nobody has been able to explain satisfactorily what this baptism was, why it was done and by whom. At least forty different solutions have been offered by scholars, but none of them have been found acceptable.[18] Without an acceptable solution it is impossible to say precisely what Paul meant in 1 Corinthians 15:29. Generally speaking, Christians have therefore been prepared to pass over this text without giving it a modern meaning that we should apply today. No orthodox Christian group has, for example, (unlike the Mormons) instituted a rite of baptism for the dead. This tells us something very significant: where we are unable to determine what a text meant, we should not attempt to say that it means something today.

But of course most texts are not as difficult as 1 Corinthians 15:29. Generally speaking, we do have a pretty good idea (particularly if we are prepared to pay attention to good scholarship) of what they meant. Although we may not be completely sure about what exactly they meant, we can describe a fairly limited range of possible meanings. To take another example from Paul, Philippians 4:22 reads, 'All the saints greet you, especially those of Caesar's household.' Here, the Christians at Philippi could

[18] See Fee, *1 Corinthians* NICNT, p. 762.

have attached a small range of meanings to 'Caesar's household': members of the emperor's family (most unlikely), members of the imperial court at Rome (not very likely), members of the imperial service somewhere else in the Roman empire from where Paul is writing (most likely).

This is quite a common situation with biblical passages. There is a small range of things that they could have meant, with some possibilities more likely than others. Yet another example is the phrase, 'the kingdom of God'. There are three main possible meanings for the word 'kingdom': 1. the realm over which a monarch reigns; 2. the people over whom he reigns; 3. the actual rule or reign itself. In fact all three meanings occur in the New Testament. The kingdom of God is the earthly people of the kingdom in Revelation 1:6 and 5:10. Occasionally it is the realm over which God reigns: e.g. Luke 16:16. Often, it is God's rule breaking in to bring change: e.g. Matthew 12:28. On the basis of these aspects, the kingdom of God might be defined as 'the sovereign rule of God manifested in Christ to defeat his enemies, creating a people over whom He reigns, and issuing in a realm or realms in which the power of his reign is manifested'.[19]

But these two examples, of 'Caesar's household' and of 'the kingdom of God' differ significantly. For 'Caesar's household' we have listed three possible meanings which are mutually incompatible. That is, the phrase means either one thing or the other or the other, and we cannot be sure which. But it does not mean all three. With 'the kingdom of God', on the other hand, we have listed three meanings which all do apply, as the definition shows. The former kind of possibilities arise from our incomplete knowledge about the Bible, while the latter arise from the richness of the Bible's theology and language.

(2) Authority

The existence of these two types of possibilities means that there is enormous variety in Bible interpretation. Christians can and do reach enormously varying conclusions about the meaning of

[19] G.E. Ladd, 'Kingdom of God' in M.C. Tenney (ed.), *The Zondervan Pictorial Bible Dictionary*, 3rd edn., p. 466.

texts for us today. They differ both because of our deficiency in knowledge and because of the richness of the Bible. But the key fact is that both sources of variation are constrained by the original sense of the text. Our deficiency of knowledge does not mean that anything goes. We do not say that, because we are unsure exactly what a text meant, it might mean anything at all. Nor do we say that, because the Bible is rich in meaning, it means anything we want.

It follows that whatever claim is made about what the Bible means for us today must take account of the possibilities defined by the original sense. Anybody, for example, who wishes to claim *on the authority of the Bible* that they know what the kingdom of God means today, will need to take account of the three aspects mentioned above. If they do not do so, perhaps claiming that the kingdom of God has nothing to do with God's rule on earth, but instead indicates a future unearthly heaven, then they will lose the right to claim they are being biblical.

This is where the idea of biblical authority must take effect in practice. When we interpret the Bible we must discipline ourselves to show how our interpretation is related to the original sense of the text. If we do not do that, then there is little point in using the Bible at all. If we are unwilling to do this, then we would be better to simply say whatever we wish without ever referring to the Bible.

This does not mean that we are limited to constantly repeating the original sense. Far from it. We must seek continually to apply the Bible in new and profound ways to our ever-changing world, and we must pray for the Spirit's help in doing that. But if it is truly to be the Bible that we apply, and not our own opinions, then we must allow ourselves to be constrained by the original sense.

(3) 'Pentecostal' Interpretation

We have seen that for most Christians, what the Bible means today must bear a particular kind of relation to what the Bible originally meant. Bible interpretation must be constrained by the original sense of the text. In this context, we now consider what Mark Stibbe says about this issue:

Stibbe agrees that the original sense does have a place in interpretation, but for him it does not have the paramount position. He asks, 'Where in the Bible does it say that the Bible merely consists of uncovering the original meaning of the author in the original situation?'[20] For him, this does not just mean that we must go on to find new and profound applications for the Bible but means that, for the Spirit-filled interpreter, the original sense is much less important. He offers the way the Old Testament is treated in the New as proof of this:

> If one examines the ways in which the New Testament preachers and authors use the Old Testament, one thing becomes immediately clear: Neither are primarily interested in what the real author meant in his *Sitz im Leben* (life-setting). In fact, they show very little concern for that. They are far more interested in what God is doing right now, and in finding Scriptures which illuminate that. In short, they are more concerned with what is called a THIS-IS-THAT approach to interpretation.[21]

This view of the way the New Testament interprets the Old is open to question (see below). But Stibbe goes on to claim that 'Pentecostals contend that a THIS-IS-THAT approach is . . . also the way in which we should interpret the Scriptures today'.[22] In a while I will return to the question of Old Testament interpretation in the New Testament. How true is this statement?

First, it is worth noting that, contrary to the impression given by the above statement, Stibbe does not speak for the majority of Pentecostals. If any single view is dominant among Pentecostal Christians, it is probably one quite close to the conservative evangelical view which Stibbe opposes (though with a greater role assigned to the 'illumination' which the Spirit gives). Among Pentecostal theologians, though, there are many different views about interpreting Scripture. However, most of them would ascribe greater importance to the original sense than he seems to allow.

---

20 *Refreshing*, p. 4.
21 Ibid., p. 5.
22 Ibid., p. 5.

In fact, generally speaking, Stibbe himself gives a higher place to the original sense than we might expect. *Times of Refreshing* contains surprisingly few examples of 'This-is-that' interpretation (the main one being of Ezekiel 47), and a great many cases using a more 'conventional' interpretation, based on the original sense. It is significant that throughout the book Stibbe refers to the Greek words lying behind the English translations. This makes sense only if he wants to understand better the original meaning. He also refers to *what Paul meant* in 1 Corinthians and *what John meant* in 1 John when they describe how to test charismatic phenomena.

An excellent example of making the original sense of prime importance is Stibbe's interpretation of the meaning of 'blasphemy against the Holy Spirit'. Here he follows the procedure recommended above of asking first what the phrase originally meant and then applying that to the current situation. Thus he answers the question, What is blasphemy against the Holy Spirit? by asking e.g. why Mark, Matthew and Luke placed the saying about blasphemy where they did in their Gospels. He concludes that 'For Mark and Matthew . . . blaspheming against the Holy Spirit means describing the works of the Spirit as evil',[23] while Luke, by contrast, 'understands the same sin as failing to witness to others once we have been filled with the Holy Spirit'.[24]

Having discovered these original senses, Stibbe attempts a contemporary application. In doing this he uses the 'classical' method described above, in which the current meaning of a text is related to but different from its original meaning. I have examined the details of his interpretation elsewhere,[25] but the significant point for the present purpose is that in this case the original sense (rightly) constrains his interpretation.

The question arises: what is the relationship between this kind of interpretation and the 'This-is-that' approach such as he uses with Ezekiel 47? Unfortunately, Stibbe is very unclear about this. It seems that his practice of what he calls 'Pentecostal

[23] *Refreshing*, p. 174.
[24] Ibid., p. 176.
[25] See my book, *Testing the Fire.*

hermeneutics' includes both the more conventional approach and the 'This-is-that' approach. He applies the Bible in the same way as other Christians do, but for him 'Pentecostal hermeneutics' has an additional element, which is what he calls 'prophetic in character'.[26] In this 'prophetic mode', the interpreter apparently need no longer be constrained by original sense and, presumably under the inspiration of the Holy Spirit, is able to offer a meaning of Scripture which is neither indicated by nor controlled by the original sense.

Nevertheless, the original sense does have a function: '. . . often-times a prophetic sense of THIS-IS-THAT comes as the Spirit-filled interpreter discovers a surprising accord between the situation of the biblical author and the present situation of his community'.[27] If the only function of the original sense is to highlight a 'surprising accord', that function seems to be relatively minor. This presumably explains why Stibbe's interpretation of Ezekiel 47, includes a number of assertions which, although they use the words of the text, have almost no basis in it.

We have already seen reasons for rejecting Stibbe's major claim that Ezekiel 47 provides a pattern which the 'Toronto Blessing' is following. Now we shall consider two of his subclaims, which illustrate the problems raised by his method. For example, he notes that Pentecostalism is a movement which has reached the peoples that the historic churches have not, people who are poor and marginalized, and he also notes that Ezekiel 47:3 speaks of the water being ankle-deep. In this connection he says:

> It may be that some significance may be drawn from this, for this wave washed the feet of those whom the historic churches were by and large not touching. This first wave was a foot-washing wave. Here the *me 'opsayim* ('water of ankles') of Ezekiel 47:3 washed the feet of the outcast, the impoverished and the marginalized.[28]

---

[26] *Refreshing*, p. 5.
[27] Ibid., p. 7.
[28] Ibid., p. 15.

This is an assertion based on word-association, and bears no relation to the original sense of Ezekiel 47:3. There is simply no indication in the text that when Ezekiel wrote about the water being ankle-deep he was thinking either of foot-washing or of the poor and marginalized. All that can be said on the basis of the original sense is that 'ankle-deep' was meant to indicate the first and shallowest stage of the water.

Here is another similar example:

> There are trees on each side of the river produced by the fourth wave (v. 7). This reminds me of Psalm 1, and the tree planted by streams of living water which symbolizes the person who meditates faithfully on God's Word. The trees in Ezekiel 47:7 are therefore a symbol of a people who are not forgetful of the Word.[29]

Once again Stibbe has cut himself free from the original sense, in which the trees symbolize, not people who remember the Word, but the new life brought by the river flowing from the temple of God.

Stibbe's interpretation of Ezekiel 47 is characterized by this freedom from the original sense. It raises the question: what status ought to be assigned to such an interpretation?

We have seen that there is contradiction in Stibbe's own statements here. Sometimes it seems that what he is offering is to be treated like any other charismatic prophecy, which can use biblical language and imagery but which does not thereby claim equal authority with interpretations of the Bible based on the original sense. Such charismatic prophecy is usually treated as being subject to and therefore lesser than biblical revelation. Surely such prophecy should not be called Bible interpretation, but simply prophecy. However, Stibbe claims that he is offering 'interpretation', and apparently ascribes to it a status equal to (or perhaps higher than?) Bible interpretation based on the original sense.

Thus, in a section entitled 'Divine Judgement', he says that the pools and marshes of Ezekiel 47.11, are:

---

[29] *Refreshing*, p. 24.

> the churches which have become bogged down. They may be churches which have become bogged down in rigid, formal, lifeless traditions. They may also be churches which have been renewed but which have become bogged down in their own version of 'lifeless tradition'. They are most likely to be churches where the leadership exercise a doctrinal control over congregations — where the doctrine in question is hostile to the experience of the Holy Spirit in power today. *So this verse contains a frightening warning.*[30]

I have italicized the final words to emphasize that Stibbe is indeed using the text to issue an authoritative warning. There are people who, he thinks, are 'hostile to the experience of the Holy Spirit in power today' and who are going to be subjected to divine judgment. This is not simply an edifying exposition. It is a 'prophetic' interpretation, supposedly made in the power of the Spirit, which appears to claim that God is issuing this warning through the text.

Remarkably, in this case the interpretation is not only free from constraint by the original sense, but actually seems to oppose it. In his commentary on Ezekiel, Leslie Allen translates verse 11 as, 'But its marshes and pools will be left impure and used to supply salt'.[31] In Ezekiel's time, salt was a very precious commodity. It was needed both for ordinary living and for worship rituals (e.g. Ezekiel 43:24). If the river had made everywhere pure and fresh, no salt would have been available. Thus according to the original sense, and completely contrary to that proposed by Stibbe, the marshes and pools (or swamps) are good things, not bad.

It is difficult to see how Scripture can be counted as authoritative in this sort of 'This-is-that' interpretation, even though it is allegedly 'interpretation' of the biblical text. The 'interpreter' seems free to say almost whatever he or she wants (or thinks the Spirit wants) while not letting the text itself have control over what is said. When that happens, the Bible is being given a fairly lowly place, despite all protestations to the contrary.

---

[30] *Refreshing*, p. 28.

[31] L.C. Allen, *Ezekiel 20–48*, p. 271.

(4) Pneumatic Interpretation

Interpretation which uses the biblical text, but which seems uncontrolled by the text, is not a new phenomenon in church history. Stibbe recognizes that it has been practised throughout the centuries, noting that 'a purely spiritual form of interpretation would result at best in allegory and at worst in the kind of super-spiritual interpretations associated with the Gnostic heresies in the early Church'.[32] The Greek word for 'spiritual' is *pneumatikos*, and so this kind of interpretation has often been called 'pneumatic interpretation'.

Stibbe claims that his 'This-is-that' approach should not be placed in this category, but it appears to carry the marks of pneumatic interpretation. It is interpretation carried out in the name of the Spirit and cut free from control by the text. As we have seen, it is tested, not by textual criteria, but by such tests as whether the same thing is being said by others (presumably under the assumption that the 'others' are also inspired by the Spirit). Stibbe thinks this is particularly convincing if the 'others' have 'had no contact with each other'.[33]

The example he gives concerns a sermon based on his interpretation of Ezekiel 47, which he delivered a few weeks after a similar sermon had been preached by another man at the same church. When people pointed out this 'coincidence', he replied, 'What's going on is that two people may be hearing similar things from the Lord.'[34] He apparently considers this to be a strong indication that his interpretation is valid, and believes it is *a key question* whether the same thing is being said by others.[35]

This appears to be a highly irresponsible procedure. Let us suppose that when the first preacher delivered his sermon on Ezekiel 47 the congregation was hearing this interpretation for the first time, so at that stage the same thing was not being said by others. Consequently, they would have had to apply other tests to the sermon. Since 'the same thing' had not yet been said 'by others', members of the congregation would have been right

[32] *Refreshing*, p. 7.
[33] Ibid., p. 6.
[34] Ibid., pp. 6–7.
[35] Ibid., p. 6.

to raise similar objections to the objections I have raised. At least some of them might thus have concluded that the sermon was in error and that the 'Toronto Blessing' is not in Ezekiel 47.

However, following the procedure recommended by Stibbe, those people would have had to change their mind once Stibbe had come and preached his sermon (assuming they happened to be present that Sunday!). They would have had to change their mind despite the fact that the reasons for concluding the previous sermon was in error would also apply to the current one. This seems highly irresponsible. If an interpretation of a text is not justified by the text, that will remain the case no matter how many times the interpretation is repeated by different people. Repetition of error, even when it is given in the name of the Spirit, remains error.

For these reasons, I think Stibbe's 'This-is-that' approach should be regarded as a type of unacceptable pneumatic interpretation. This is true even though he thinks he has guarded himself against 'super-spiritual interpretations' by not neglecting 'the kinds of questions which are posed by historical critics'.[36] His own interpretation of Ezekiel 47 shows that an interest in 'issues of history' does not guarantee this. He offers two paragraphs of background historical information about Ezekiel and his situation as a prophet living in exile. But when it comes to his interpretation of the text, the historical information seems to make no difference at all. Stibbe does not, for example, use the historical information to understand what Ezekiel might have intended the marshes and pools to symbolize. Instead he simply asserts that they symbolize 'bogged down churches'.

3. Interpretation in the New Testament

At this point we return to the question of how the Old Testament is interpreted in the New. Is it the case that Stibbe's approach finds justification there, as he claims?

First of all, we need to acknowledge that there are some very real differences between the way the New Testament interprets the Old and accepted contemporary practice. Stibbe is right to

---

36 *Refreshing*, p. 7.

say that the New Testament preachers and authors showed less concern for the original sense than we often do. As we will see, there are indeed interpretations of Old Testament texts in the New Testament which, methodologically speaking, have considerable similarities with the kind of thing Stibbe has done with Ezekiel 47.

However, Stibbe's simple conclusion that, because something is done in the New Testament, we should do likewise, does not necessarily follow. It fails to take account both of why the New Testament authors reached the interpretations they did and why Christians thought it necessary to collect together the books of the New Testament and make them part of the Bible. In technical terms, it fails both to take account of differences in interpretative method and to take seriously the issue of canonicity.

(1) Canonicity and the Original Sense

Put rather simplistically, the books of the New Testament became part of the Christian canon as a substitute for the authoritative presence of the disciples who had known Jesus. In the first century and the early part of the second, the young Christian churches were able to shape their lives with the help of people who had known Jesus. But, as those people began to die, the need arose for authoritative written documents which would enable the churches to continue to shape their lives in a way faithful to Jesus and to the teachings of those Jesus had authorized to continue his work. Without such documents, there would be no means of deciding between actions and beliefs that were genuinely Christian and those which were not. Our New Testament is the result of deliberations among the churches as to which documents should be assigned this normative status. (It is worth noting that the word 'canon' expresses this idea: the Greek term *kanon* means literally 'measuring rod', hence the canon is the body of literature by which we measure our faith.)

It follows that, in order to be consistent with the reasons why the New Testament canon came into being, the church's interpretation of the New Testament should primarily be devoted to discovering the teachings and life of our Lord and the teachings of the apostles, and to applying these to the life of the church.

That is why most Christians have come to regard the original sense as of paramount importance. It is by interpreting the documents according to their original sense that we are able to understand what their authors wanted to say about these matters.

There are many other ways in which the New Testament documents might be treated. It is possible to treat them, for instance, as sources for historical and sociological reconstruction of life in the earliest church. This is a valid approach, and can greatly aid our understanding, but it will not directly help the church decide matters of faith and action. Another (in my view, less valid) treatment would be that taken by various cult leaders who disregard the original sense entirely and apply various texts from the New Testament to themselves and their 'new religions'. As a body of literature, the New Testament is like any other: it can be (and indeed has been) used to justify almost anything. However, if we are to be faithful to the decision of the early church that these particular documents are to be our canon, then we must also be faithful to the *way* in which they were supposed to be canon. That is, as documents which, when read according to their original sense, tell us about the teachings and life of our Lord and the teachings of his chosen apostles.

Thus, even those parts of the New Testament which show little concern for the original sense of the documents they are interpreting, *we* rightly interpret according to the original sense of the New Testament writer. For example, in 1 Corinthians 14:21 Paul quotes Isaiah 28:11 as part of his discussion of the gift of tongues. The original sense of Isaiah 28:11 is that, because Israel has refused to listen to God's requirements, God will send a message of judgment to the Jews by allowing invasion by a foreign people, the Assyrians; God's 'messengers', speaking an alien tongue. Paul, on the other hand, uses the verse to speak about the gift of tongues in churches, a different matter entirely, and seems to ignore the original sense. However, we only understand Paul rightly by asking what he originally meant by his interpretation, what the original sense of 1 Corinthians 14:21 is. The fact that in his treatment of Isaiah 28:11 Paul is unconcerned with the original sense, does not justify us in being unconcerned with Paul's original sense.

My point is that, if we are to treat the New Testament as authoritative, we must interpret it according to its original sense. If we do otherwise, we are ignoring the reasons why it became part of the canon.

(2) 'Prophetic Interpretation' of the Old Testament

Having said that, it is obvious that the matter is somewhat different with interpretation of the Old Testament. Is it not possible that we ought to be constrained by the original sense when interpreting the New, but not when interpreting the Old? Might it be that, because the same Holy Spirit is in us who was in the New Testament preachers and authors, we can interpret the Old Testament in the same way as they did? In order to answer this question, we need to consider what I called earlier the issue of differences in interpretative method. This will take some time but will clarify an important point.

4. Differences in Interpretative Method

It is important to realize that the writers of the New Testament documents were Jews who had been schooled in the Jewish methods of Scripture interpretation. The interpretations of the Old Testament that we see in the New follow these methods, differing only from other Jewish interpretations in that they have specifically Christian content. It is worth spending a little time looking more closely at this matter.

The collective name for the different methods of ancient Jewish interpretation is *midrash*. In his book, *What is Midrash?*, Jacob Neusner distinguishes three main types of *midrash*:

> In *paraphrase* the exegete of the Hebrew Scriptures will state in other words the self-evident and ordinary sense of the Hebrew. Much of the Targumim[37] render in Aramaic a fairly straightforward version of the Hebrew, though the line between the simple sense and interpretation is not infrequently crossed.

[37] 'Targumim' is the name for translations that were made of the Hebrew Scriptures into Aramaic.

> In *prophecy* the exegete will read Scripture as an account of things that are now happening or are going to happen. In general, the more common approach was the second: 'This verse refers to that event.' Scripture was taken to provide an account of the present and near-term future. The *Pesherim*[38] of the Essene library at Qumran and passages of Matthew . . . show how *midrash* works as prophecy.
>
> In *parable* the exegete will read Scripture as an account of what the words say but with deeper meanings . . . Important Christian exegetes of Scripture, especially Matthew and Paul, present examples of reading Scripture as allegory or parable . . . [but also] the vast rabbinic corpus of *midrash*-collection readily illustrates this approach.[39]

Midrash, in other words, was practised by Christian Jews and non-Christian Jews alike. What is more — and this is very important — the New Testament writers interpreted the Old Testament according to midrashic methods for the simple reason that those were the methods they had learned to use in their upbringing as Jews.

For the purposes of our discussion, the key thing to realize about Midrash is that its methods of interpretation were *not particularly interested in the original sense*. We can see this by looking at two examples. First, the Aramaic translation known as Targum Neofiti paraphrases Genesis 3:15 as follows (words in roman are the actual words of Genesis 3:15 while those in italics are added by the writer of the Targum):

> And I will put hostility between you and the woman,
> and between your children and her children.
>
> *And when her children guard the Torah and keep the commandments they will aim against you and* strike you on your head *and kill you.*
>
> *And when they forsake the commandments of the Torah, you will take aim and* bite them on their heels *and cause them to sicken.*

---

[38] *'Pesherim'* is the name for interpretations or explanations of a verse of Scripture, according to which a given statement in the text is identified with an event or personality in the present time.

[39] J. Neusner, *What is Midrash?*, pp. 1–2.

> *However, there will be a cure for her children, but for you there will be no cure. For in the future they will find relief in the Remnant [of Israel?] in the day of the king Messiah.*[40]

Here, Genesis 3:15, whose original sense has to do with the effects of the Fall, is made to be about the effects of studying and practising (or not studying and not practising) Torah.

Second, in one of the Dead Sea scrolls we find the following commentary on Habakkuk 2:17 (again, the words in roman are the actual words of Habakkuk 2:17 while those in italics are from the writer of the scroll):

> *Interpreted, this saying concerns the Wicked Priest, inasmuch as he shall be paid the reward which he himself tended to the Poor. For* Lebanon *is the Council of the Community; and the* beasts *are the Simple of Judah who keep the Law. As he himself plotted the destruction of the Poor, so will God condemn him to destruction. As for that which He said,* Because of the blood of the city and the violence done to the land: *interpreted,* the city *is Jerusalem where the wicked priest committed abominable deeds and defiled the Temple of God.* The violence done to the land: *these are the cities of Judah where he robbed the Poor of their possessions.*[41]

Again, the original sense of Habakkuk 2:17 is ignored, and the verse is interpreted as referring to the Qumran community (of which the commentator is a member) and of events of the commentator's time.

The Dead Sea scrolls are writings from a period before the New Testament (first to second century BCE), while the targums come from a later period (fourth century AD onward). The New Testament, therefore, fits into a continuum of time in which people who interpreted Holy Scriptures were most often not interested in the original sense.

There is a reason for adducing all this evidence. It shows that the writers of the New Testament interpreted the Old Testament in the way they did, and in particular with little regard to the original sense, not because they thought, for example, that that

---

40 *What is Midrash?*, p. 29.
41 Ibid., p. 34.

was how the Holy Spirit was telling them to do it, but simply because that was the way that, as Jews, they had learned to treat the Scriptures. This is not to say that the Holy Spirit was not involved in the process which led to the writing of the New Testament. But, in equating his kind of interpretation of Ezekiel 47 with New Testament interpretation of the Old, Mark Stibbe seems to me to be being a little disingenuous. He ignores the fact that lack of interest in the original sense was due primarily to the methods of interpretation that Matthew and Paul, for example, had been schooled in and seems to imply that it is directly due to some sort of inward guidance from the Holy Spirit. He seems to imply that the Holy Spirit was whispering in their ears, 'I know the original sense tells you the text means this, but I am telling you it really means that'.

Quite simply, this has nothing to with the actual situation. In New Testament times, Christians and non-Christians alike were not particularly interested in being constrained by the original sense. It will be helpful now to look a little more carefully at just what the New Testament writers *were* interested in.

5. Christological Interpretation

The preachers and authors of the New Testament are our fellow Christians. We and they have much in common. But it is important to realize also that they stood at a unique place in history with a unique apprehension of what God has done in Jesus Christ. They had direct access to the foundational events of Christianity, an access which we can only have indirectly, through what they tell us.

It was in the light of their unique situation that they interpreted the Old Testament. For example, when, immediately after Pentecost, Peter told his hearers, 'This is what was spoken by the prophet Joel', and proceeded to quote and interpret Joel 2:28–32, he did so with unique authority (an authority which we are wise not to try to match). Peter was declaring that the foundational events of Christianity are the fulfilment of the Hebrew scriptures. The same is true when Matthew, for example, reports Mary's flight to Egypt with the baby Jesus, and says,

'This was to fulfil what the Lord had spoken by the prophet, "Out of Egypt have I called my son".'

This last example is a good one because, while Peter's interpretation of Joel appears to be constrained to quite some degree by the original sense, that is not so with Matthew. Matthew quotes the second half of Hosea 11:1. The whole of Hosea 11:1 reads, 'When Israel was a child, I loved him, and out of Egypt I called my son.' According to the original sense this is a description of a past event, not a prophecy of a future one. It tells how in the past God brought the people of Israel out of exile in Egypt and made them his nation, treating Israel as a son. Nor does it speak of a literal son, but of a metaphorical one, of Israel *as* a son. If Matthew had felt constrained by the original sense, presumably he would not have offered the interpretation he did offer. Clearly, Matthew interpreted the Old Testament according to the midrashic methods we looked at earlier. (Neusner gives plenty of other examples of midrashic interpretation in Matthew's Gospel.[42])

However, it is important that, in distinction from other Jewish interpretation, Matthew sought to give his interpretation christological content. His concern was to show that in Jesus Christ was to be found the fulfilment of the Old Testament. For Matthew and his readers, the methods of interpretation he used to show this were entirely normal and acceptable. But this does not automatically justify us in doing the same sort of thing.

6. Is Midrash Appropriate for us Today?

The first point I wish to make is that anybody who wishes to justify using a midrashic interpretation by means of parallels with the New Testament ought to take seriously what it is that is special about New Testament interpretation of the Old, namely its *christological focus*, rather than what is common to the New Testament and other literature of the period, namely its lack of interest in the original sense. Christological focus surely is the outstanding feature of New Testament interpretation of the Old. Consequently, it would have been truer to the New

---

[42] See *What is Midrash?*, pp. 37–8.

Testament if Stibbe's interpretation of Ezekiel 47 had been christological. One might, for example, interpret the temple of Ezekiel 47 as representing Jesus Christ, and the river as representing that stream of new life which flows out from Jesus into all the world as the Holy Spirit awakens men and women to faith in Christ. By contrast, Stibbe seems to focus on the details of what he sees happening in the church and world today and what he thinks is going to happen in the future. Rather than being christological, his interpretation is ecclesiological and futurological.

We are left with the question of whether, even if used with a christological focus, midrashic methods are appropriate for us today. Our earlier discussion of canonicity gave reasons for considering them to be inappropriate for interpretation of the New Testament; but what of the Old Testament?

The key thing to realize is that Matthew and the other New Testament authors had come to the conviction that the foundational Christian events — Jesus' life, death and resurrection, and the subsequent outpouring of the Spirit — were the fulfilment of all God had been doing in and through Israel, and therefore were the fulfilment of the Jewish Scriptures. As we have seen, Jews had a number of different methods of interpreting those Scriptures, and they tended not to be constrained by the original sense. So Matthew and the other New Testament authors sought to show that, even when read according to those methods, the foundational events could be discerned in the Old Testament.

This does not mean that such an approach is justified today. We are in a completely different situation from that of the New Testament authors. First, many of the interpretative methods practised two thousand years ago are not in use today. Matthew, Paul and the other New Testament writers were writing for people who understood and accepted midrash. There is little point in Christians using such methods today. Using them is only likely to lead to incomprehension or worse.

Secondly, Christians today are not required to prove that the events we are experiencing now are the fulfilment of the Jewish scriptures. This is a very important issue. We must not put current experiences on a par with the foundational Christian events. Nor must we claim the same kind of authoritative understanding of current events as the first disciples possessed. It is a mistake, for example, to place our apprehension of the 'Toronto Blessing' on a par with the disciples' apprehension of Pentecost. Jesus specifically told the disciples to wait in Jerusalem for the promise of the Father, baptism in the Holy Spirit (Acts 1:4–5). Consequently, when they experienced Pentecost, they had direct teaching from Jesus explain it. Jesus did not also say that in two thousand years the 'Toronto Blessing' would come as the Father had promised. So, while Peter had good reason to say that the Pentecost experience was promised by God and so the fulfilment of the Scriptures, we do not have good reason to do the same with the 'Toronto Blessing'. That is true whether the 'Toronto Blessing' is 'of God' or not.

We have arrived at a point of general importance. The basic problem with Stibbe's 'prophetic interpretation', his 'This-is-that' approach, is that it fails to take account of the changing role of the Old Testament and of the difference between our situation and that of the New Testament authors. That the Old Testament has had a changing role is obvious. Its primary (though not exclusive) role for Jews at the time of Jesus was as a source of Law according to which they were to live. With the coming of Christ, the importance of that role diminished and another became primary. For the earliest Christians, the Old Testament came to be that which predicted Christ (or, in the language I have been using, that which predicted 'the foundational Christian events'), and so, in a sense, that which predicted the earliest Christians' current experience. It also functioned as that which related how God characteristically acted and what it meant to be the people of God. So, for example, Hebrews 11 uses Old Testament examples to explain what it means to be people of faith.

For modern Christians, this latter function tends to be the most important. The Old Testament describes how God acted in the past and what it meant to be his people. In some ways the experience of Christians today will be similar to that of people in the Old Testament. Many of the Psalms, for example, speak to Christians about their own spirituality, not just the spirituality of the psalmist. But this does not mean the Old Testament *predicts* our experience in the way it predicted the foundational Christian events. And, of course, we understand what the Old Testament tells us about how God acted in the past and what it meant to be his people, when we read the Old Testament constrained by the original sense.

It follows from this that it is neither necessary nor appropriate to try to interpret the Old Testament as specifically predicting our current experiences. That is not its role. It is particularly inappropriate when such interpretation entails to the kinds of speculative and even fanciful procedures offered by Stibbe. The way Christians should read the Old Testament is as a collection of documents written by the people of God about their experiences of God and their faith in him. We will be able to understand what they have to say to us about these things only if we spend time trying to understand what they originally intended to say. The way to do this is by interpreting the texts according to their original sense.

7. Conclusion

Christians hold the Bible in high regard, so when something is claimed to be 'scriptural' or 'biblical' it tends to be taken very seriously. In the Christian church, assertions based on Bible interpretation are given considerable authority. For that reason, we need ways of checking that the Bible interpretations offered are properly grounded in the biblical text. In other words, adequate hermeneutics are vital. Adequate, or even good, hermeneutics will not, of course, guarantee good interpretations. A number of other elements need to be present for that to happen. But a good interpretation will have behind it good hermeneutics. On the other hand, bad hermeneutics, like bad ingredients in a cake, will lead to bad results. For this reason, I believe it is important to reject Stibbe's 'This-is-that' approach. It is an approach which, even while using the biblical text, prevents the Bible from speaking its message to us, and causes us instead to read our own messages into it.

Bibliography

Allen, L.C., *Ezekiel 20–48* WBC (Dallas: Word Books, 1990)
Fee, G., *1 Corinthians*, NICNT (Grand Rapids: Eerdmans, 1987).

Ladd, G.E., 'Kingdom of God' in M.C. Tenney (ed.), *The Zondervan Pictorial Bible Dictionary* (Grand Rapids: Zondervan, 1967[3]).
Neusner, J., *What is Midrash?* (Philadelphia: Fortress Press, 1987).
Smith, M.D.J., *Testing the Fire: A Biblical Analysis of the 'Toronto Blessing'* (Cambridge: St Matthew's Press, 1996).
Stibbe, M., *Times of Refreshing: A Practical Theology of Revival for Today* (London: Marshall Pickering, 1995).

Chapter 3
Ecstatic Laughter

Much of the publicity given to the 'Toronto Blessing' has resulted from the physical phenomena associated with it. For the secular media these are 'what it's all about'. Some Christians are scandalized by them; others tend to dismiss them as 'superficial'. But it is obvious that any discussion of the Blessing must take them seriously. In his book, Mark Stibbe recognizes this by including a chapter entitled 'Extraordinary Phenomena'. In it he pinpoints 'four vital questions' which must be asked about unusual phenomena accompanying 'a new move of the Holy Spirit'. Interestingly, although the chapter title refers to 'experiences' it focuses exclusively on laughter, a subject which Stibbe clearly regards as very important.

The four questions are:

1. What is the nature of these experiences?
2. Are they biblical?
3. Have we witnessed them before in church history?
4. What purpose do they serve?[1]

This chapter considers questions 2 and 3, beginning with question 3.

1. Laughter in Church History

The accumulated experience of the church over the centuries is a valuable resource. In studying it there is wisdom to be acquired and there are lessons to be learned. But it is not clear how Stibbe intends this appeal to church history to function in the present

1 *Refreshing*, p. 104.

case. If the answer to the church history question (No. 3) is 'No, we have not witnessed this phenomenon before', this would apparently not entail ruling it out. On page 85 he insists that 'we cannot dictate to God how he is to act in a particular situation', which presumably means that church history cannot dictate to him either. If on the other hand the answer is 'Yes, we have witnessed it before' — and if the sheer fact of its having happened is sufficient to authenticate it — then the history of the church could never deliver a negative judgment on anything and there would be no point in asking the question. For this question to be meaningful, more must be required than for a thing simply to have happened. And in fact it is obvious that not everything which has happened in the history of the church can automatically merit approval. It must be the case that any particular aspect of the church's life in the past is to be judged acceptable on its merits, and on the same terms as aspects of the church's life in the present.

Elsewhere Stibbe says that the basis of such a judgment must be the Bible, which he asserts must be our guide[2] and is 'the inspired and authoritative revelation of God's nature and God's acts'.[3] I agree, and suggest that the value of church history in a case such as this consists in the opportunity to benefit from the insights of Christian leaders who witnessed past events, provided that these leaders were well versed in the Bible. It seems strange that Stibbe does not avail himself of this resource.

When discussing the phenomenon of laughter, Stibbe appeals for support to two of the great periods of revival in particular. They are the Evangelical Awakening in eighteenth-century England and the Great Awakening in New England, America, which began at about the same time. John Wesley, one of the leaders of the Evangelical Awakening, described those whom he witnessed in the grip of the unusual phenomenon of laughter as 'buffeted of Satan'.[4] Stibbe gives reasons for dismissing this judgment. The first is that Wesley had himself previously experienced the phenomenon. But surely a man

2 Ibid. p. 110.
3 Ibid. p. xii.
4 Wesley's Journal, (May 9 1740); *Refreshing*, p. 133.

may have an experience which he later finds reason to disclaim? The second reason is Stibbe's belief (for which he offers no evidence and which is couched in terms of 'I believe' and 'it may be') that Wesley was influenced by the social conventions and cultural norms of his time, that he had 'bought into the values of respectability'.[5] But was Wesley especially likely to succumb to the influence of convention? In stepping outside the regulations of the Anglican Church and taking to the fields to preach the gospel he defied convention and shocked society in a startling way. Nor is someone who has 'bought into the values of respectability' likely to court the possibility of being pelted with mud and stones.

There is also some inconsistency in what Stibbe says about the influence of contemporary culture on Wesley. On the one hand, he describes eighteenth-century society as being characterized by a 'respectability' which regarded loud laughter as 'socially undignified', and attributes Wesley's rejection of laughter to social conformity. Yet immediately afterwards, he suggests that Wesley's attitude to laughter was due to his concern about the *frivolity* of English society and was a reaction *against* the 'sense of abandonment, joviality and fun' which many adopted. And indeed in a previous chapter of *Times of Refreshing* ('Cultural Factors', pp 86ff.) Stibbe presents evidence of widespread drunkenness and violence affecting all strata of eighteenth-century society, such that there was 'something wildly Dionysian' about this period. At the time when Wesley rejected ecstatic laughter, Britain was a 'nation high on every kind of addiction'. This description does not accord with the picture of a society committed to 'the values of respectability'. In addition to lacking corroboration, the argument here lacks consistency.

It seems strange to claim the support of an historical phenomenon while dismissing on unsubstantiated grounds the judgment of one of the foremost leaders of the movement within which it occurred. In fact, Wesley's condemnation of the phenomenon of laughter so early in his career (1740) is particularly significant, in view of the fact that he at first accepted other unusual physical

[5] *Refreshing*, p. 134.

phenomena as genuine and only later repudiated them as the work of Satan.[6] And again, his earlier acceptance of these phenomena argues against the idea that he rejected laughter because he had 'bought into the values of respectability'.

The opinions of Jonathan Edwards, who took part in the Great Awakening in New England, suffer a different fate. In order to establish Edwards as an ally and supporter of the current phenomenon of laughter, Stibbe gives a quotation which allegedly shows Edwards writing about 'the different ways in which people were moved in their "affections" during his own day'. This is how the quotation appears in Stibbe's text:

> Their joyful surprise has caused their hearts as it were to leap so that they have been ready to break forth into laughter, tears often at the same time issuing like a flood, and intermingling a loud weeping. Sometimes they have not been able to forbear crying out with a loud voice, expressing their great admiration. The manner of God's work on the soul, sometimes especially, is very mysterious.[7]

Stibbe asks readers to note particularly the last sentence when considering the unusual phenomenon of laughter. The implication is that Edwards regarded laughter as a mysterious work of God on the soul. But this particular sentence has been transposed from its original position. The source is Edwards's *Narrative of Surprising Conversions*, in which the first part of the above extract occurs on pages 37 and 38[8], but the last sentence not until two pages later on page 40. In addition, in context the words refer not to laughter, nor to any other way in which people were moved in their affections, but to the mysterious nature of the work of conversion and to the difficulty of pinpointing the exact time at which it takes place in a person's experience.

The real significance of what Edwards is saying is further concealed by the absence of any explanation of the category of

---

[6] See W Stephen Gunter, *The Limits of Love Divine, John Wesley's Response to Antinomianism and Enthusiasm* for a discussion of Wesley's attitude to strange phenomena, especially the chapter 'More Heat Than Light?' For Wesley's later condemnation of falling, screaming, crying out, see *Journal* (April 3, 1786).

[7] *Refreshing*, p. 109f.

[8] 'A Narrative of Surprising Conversions' in *Jonathan Edwards on Revival*.

people referred to. Who were 'they'? The words immediately preceding the quotation describe the people of whom Edwards is speaking as: 'having been broken with apprehension of divine wrath, and sunk into an abyss, under a sense of guilt which they were ready to think was beyond the mercy of God'.

So they were unbelievers brought under conviction of sin, not Christians, as is the case with those we are thinking about in connection with the Toronto Blessing laughter.

Finally, although Edwards says that these people were '*ready* to break forth into laughter', the phenomenon he actually describes is weeping. He is not in fact describing laughter at all.

In actual fact there is further evidence that Edwards was no supporter of ecstatic laughter. The above extract relates to the revival of 1736. In *The Distinguishing Marks of a Work of the Spirit of God*, Edwards discusses the revival of 1740–1742. This second revival was, he said, 'much purer' than the earlier one, 'more purely spiritual . . . particularly . . . in this respect, that . . . they rejoice with a more solemn, reverential, humble joy, as God directs, Psalm 2:11'. This was not because the rejoicing was less; it was greater, but 'it abases them, breaks their heart, and brings them into the dust. When they speak of their joys, it is not with laughter but with a flood of tears. Those who laughed before weep now and yet by their united testimony their joy is vastly purer and sweeter than that which did before raise their animal spirits.'[9]

Clearly Edwards did not regard laughter as a phenomenon to be sought but rather welcomed its disappearance. If further confirmation of this is needed, one last extract will provide it. It is taken from *Some Thoughts Concerning the Present Revival of Religion in New England* and describes the experience of an unnamed person, who was probably Edwards' wife, during the later revival: 'This great rejoicing has been with trembling, i.e. attended with a deep and lively sense of the greatness and majesty of God and the person's own exceeding littleness and vileness. Spiritual joys in this person never were attended with the least appearance of laughter or lightness either of countenance or manner of

[9] 'The Distinguishing Marks of a Work of the Spirit of God' in *Jonathan Edwards on Revival*, pp. 129f.

speaking, but with a peculiar abhorrence of such appearances in spiritual rejoicings.'[10] Concerning this, Edwards says, 'O that everyone's experience could be like this person's!'

We do not find in the work of Edwards support for the phenomenon of laughter. What we do find is the assertion that in considering physical phenomena, 'The nature of the operations and affections [are] to be enquired into, and examined by the rule of God's word.'[11] So we come to the second of the four questions posed by Stibbe.

2. Is it Biblical?

We have seen that the appeal to Wesley and Edwards is seriously flawed. But Stibbe is rightly (and wisely) unwilling to base his case for Toronto Blessing laughter on church history alone. Under the heading 'What does the Bible say?' he states that 'If we are to develop some theological foundations for assessing this experience we must use the Bible as our guide.'[12] This apparently signals an intention to assemble criteria for deciding whether the unusual phenomenon of laughter is biblical.[13] It will be my contention that in fact no assessment of this kind takes place.

Stibbe appears to believe that the more references one can find, the more certain one can be of having biblical support. But when we ask if something is biblical, we do not mean, 'Does the Bible mention it?' but, 'Does the Bible record that God commands, approves or sanctions it?' It is the meaning of the biblical statements that matters, not the mere presence of certain words. For example, Psalm 53:1 contains the words 'There is no God'; it is only by placing them in the context of the

---

[10] 'Some Thoughts Concerning the Present Revival of Religion in New England' in *The Works of Jonathan Edwards*, Vol 1, p. 376. I am indebted to Dr Nick Needham for drawing my attention to this passage in a talk given in June 1995.

[11] 'Distinguishing Marks', p. 94.

[12] *Refreshing*, p. 110.

[13] He follows by listing 37 verses in the Bible concerning laughter. English translations vary; the words 'laugh' and 'laughter' do not appear in all versions of the verses in Stibbe's list. Appendix C contains the verses in the versions in which they appear in Stibbe's list. My comments on the English text are based on these except where otherwise stated.

preceding 'The fool says in his heart . . .' that their significance becomes apparent.

The claim that the phenomenon of extraordinary laughter is biblical cannot be supported simply on the basis of the number of references to laughter which can be culled from the Bible. What matters is the treatment of this material and whether it can be utilized to construct a convincing biblical case.

Stibbe's central conclusion is that the Bible speaks of two types of laughter: mocking / derisive laughter and joyful laughter. He supplies a list of Old Testament references to laughter and says that the word used for mocking / derisive laughter is *gelao/gelos* and the one for joyful laughter is *sugchairo*. This word is associated with the Greek word *chara* (= 'joy').[14] These are all Greek words and he finds them in the Septuagint, the Greek translation of the Old Testament, made c. 250–150 BC. His only purpose in discussing them is to establish precise definitions which he later applies to occurrences of the same words in the New Testament. If he is wrong about their meaning then his argument at this point does nothing to support his claim that the laughter is a biblical phenomenon. We shall examine the *gelao* and *sugchairo* categories separately.

(1) Gelao

The word *gelao* is of particular interest to Stibbe because it is used in Luke 6:21: 'Blessed are you that weep now for you shall laugh' (*gelao*). He claims that the laughter referred to here is mocking, derisive laughter. The reason he gives for this is that '*gelao,* as we have already noted, most frequently connotes mocking laughter'.[15]

He justifies this by pointing to the use of *gelao* in the Septuagint. He notes however that in Greek literature from pre-classical times onwards the verb *gelao* and the noun *gelos* are used to refer both to joyful laughter and to mocking laughter, but he asserts: '[The Septuagint] almost always uses *gelao / gelos* in the sense of mocking and superior laughter. If you look in the Old Testament

[14] *Refreshing,* p. 117. *Gelao*: 'laugh' (verb); *gelos*: 'laughter' (noun).
[15] Ibid., p. 116.

references cited above, you will find this nuance of derision is often visible in the English translations.'[16]

We should note that there are *three implications* in Stibbe's argument:

a) that notwithstanding its dual sense in Greek literature, the Septuagint translators regarded *gelao* as primarily connoting mocking, derisive laughter;
b) that all the Old Testament references in Stibbe's list which have a derisive nuance contain *gelao* or *gelos* in the Septuagint;
c) that the Septuagint usage of *gelao* may be used to ascertain Luke's meaning in 6:21.

These implications repay careful study. We begin with:

Implication b) Stibbe gives a wholly wrong impression of the pattern of usage of *gelao* and *gelos* in the Septuagint. The 31 Old Testament verses which he cites contain 33 occurrences of (the English words) 'laugh' and 'laughter' (Genesis 18:5 and 21:6 each contain two). I detect a derisive tone in 23 (see Appendix A). But it simply is not the case that *gelao* or *gelos* occurs in each of these. The true pattern is more varied. Of the 23 derisive references, *gelao* accounts for only seven (and *gelos* for only one). The remaining 15 contain several different verbs: *katagelao, ekgelao, epigelao, mukterizo, empaizo* and *euphraino*.

Implication a) Is it true that the Septuagint translators regarded *gelao* as primarily denoting derisive laughter (by contrast with other words for laughter)? In attempting to answer this question we shall leave out of account words such as *mukterizo, empaizo* and *euphraino,* since they do not properly denote laughter as such (see Appendix B). We are concerned with the words which may be used to denote actual laughter — *katagelao, ekgelao* and *epigelao*. Obviously they share a common root with *gelao* but they are differentiated from it, and from each other, by their different prefixes (*kata, ek, epi*) and must be treated as separate units of vocabulary. Our survey will include those occurrences of these verbs which Stibbe's word search did not pick up.

---

[16] *Refreshing,* p. 115.

This is the pattern which emerges from our study of Greek words for laughter as used in the Septuagint:

i) *Gelao* occurs 11 times in those books in the Septuagint which are included in the Protestant canon, plus one variant reading at Job 19:17. (Of these, eight appear in Stibbe's list). Of the 12 occurrences eight are definitely derisive, two are definitely not (Job 29:24; Ecclesiastes 3:4) and two are obscure (Job 19:7; Jeremiah 20:8).
ii) *Katagelao* occurs in the canonical Septuagint 15 times (7 in Stibbe's list) and all are derisive.
iii) *Ekgelao* occurs in the canonical Septuagint five times (three in Stibbe's list) and again, all are derisive.
iv) *Epigelao* occurs once in the canonical Septuagint, as cited in Stibbe's list, and the context is derisive.
v) *Eggelao* appears as a variant reading in Psalm 2:4 where the laughter is derisive.

Thus, out of a total of 29 occasions when the Greek translators sought a verb for 'laugh derisively', they chose *gelao* only eight times; it was in fact much more likely to be ignored than included. It is also significant that *gelao* is the only verb used in a non-derisive sense.

None the less, *gelao* is used derisively eight times and only twice non-derisively. Does this support Stibbe's implication that the Septuagint translators regarded it as primarily denoting derisive laughter? I contend that it does not, for the following reason. We need to bear in mind that the Septuagint is a translation of a particular body of literature — the Hebrew Scriptures. If, as is in fact the case, the overwhelming majority of references to laughter within that literature are to derisive laughter, then the translators' opportunities to use *gelao* in a non-derisive sense were strictly limited. We may indeed conclude that they regarded it as an appropriate verb to convey the sense of derisive laughter; but the evidence of the Septuagint is not evidence that they regarded it as *unsuitable* for joyful laughter. In translating the Old Testament, they simply lacked the occasion so to use it.

In conclusion, then, we may note (i) that in seeking a verb to express derisive laughter, the Septuagint translators were more likely to avoid *gelao* than to use it; (ii) that it is the only verb used non-derisively; and (iii) that this second point is particularly significant because there were so few occasions when a non-derisive verb was required. It is clear that there are no grounds for concluding that they regarded *gelao* as primarily denoting derisive laughter. It could denote either kind, and as such they used it.

Implication c) Is Stibbe justified in thinking that Luke's use of *gelao* in 6:21 may be determined by reference to its use in the Septuagint? We have seen that there is no reason to think that the Septuagint translators regarded *gelao* as having a primarily derisive sense. But even if it were possible to maintain this it would be unsound to interpret Luke's use of *gelao* on the basis of its use in the Septuagint or in any other context elsewhere. As Stibbe himself acknowledges, *gelao* may be used in both derisive and in joyful contexts, so it is clear that the connotation of either derision or joy cannot be attributed to the presence of *gelao* itself. The derisive or joyful connotations must be due to other factors — either to the presence of other, clarifying words in the immediate context, or to the wider situational context. We can see this in Genesis 18:12; when we recognize that Sarah's laughter here is the mocking laughter of unbelief rather than of joy; this is not because *gelao* is used but because Sarah herself points out that she is past childbearing age. The nuance of mockery is not contributed by *gelao*. This illustrates the principle that the basic unit of meaning is not the word but the sentence or word-combination. Meaning resides in the combination as a whole, not in individual words. The meaning of a sentence is not the exact sum of its verbal components; rather it is the result of the way in which each component mutually restricts the semantic contribution of the others.[17]

---

[17] Take E. Nida's well known example concerning the words 'green' and 'house'. 'Green' may, in different contexts, be taken: as a colour; as denoting lack of experience; as meaning 'unripe'. 'House' may refer: to a dwelling; to a business establishment; to lineage. But when the two occur together in the sentence 'He lives in a green house', then 'green' must be taken only as a colour and 'house' only as a dwelling. The other meanings are not present in that context. (And if the two words occur together as 'greenhouse', the mutual restriction is at its greatest and 'green' makes practically no contribution at all). 'Implications of Contemporary Linguistics for Biblical Scholarship', *JBL* 91 (1972).

Although words have basic 'core' meanings (to a greater or lesser extent) their semantic contribution in any given context is determined by the relationships which they contract with other words and by the wider context. We must then allow the context to establish the sense of *gelao* in Luke 6:21; its contribution in other contexts cannot be determinative. (For Luke 6:21, see below.)

(2) Sugchairo

Stibbe bases his *sugchairo* category of 'joyful laughter' on the use of this verb in the Septuagint at Genesis 21:6b, where Sarah, speaking about the birth of Isaac, anticipates the reaction of those who will hear of the birth. The verb in the Hebrew text which describes their reaction is *tsachaq*. Almost all English versions render *tsachaq* as 'laugh'. Most (e.g., NIV, REB, GNB, AV) translate the phrase as 'will laugh with me', which suggests that Sarah's neighbours will share her own delight at Isaac's birth. RSV, however, has 'will laugh over me', which suggests that the laughter expresses a degree of amusement at Sarah's situation (cf. Gen. 18:12). Both senses are possible.

In rendering this same phrase into Greek, the Septuagint translator used the verb *sugchairo*. As we have seen, Stibbe regards *sugchairo* as 'the normal Greek word' for 'joyous laughter'; a 'verb with the word *chara* or "joy" at the heart of it'.[18] In fact, *sugchairo* is not a 'normal Greek word' for 'laugh' either in the Bible or elsewhere; indeed, it is not a word for 'laugh' at all. Genesis 21:6 is its sole occurrence in the canonical books of the Septuagint[19] and in Greek literature as a whole its range of meaning is 'rejoice with', 'wish one joy', 'congratulate', 'wish one joy of'. 'Laugh' is not among the available possibilities. We may note two things concerning the Septuagint translator's use of *sugchairo*. The first is that he understands the text in the same way as a number of other translators, including the NIV, NRSV and NEB and other translations (those who hear of Isaac's birth will share Sarah's joy).

---

[18] *Refreshing*, p. 117.

[19] In the non-canonical books it occurs once in a variant reading at 3 Maccabees 1:8, as against a majority reading of chairo (rejoice).

The second point to note is that the translator renders the general sense of this interpretation by using a verb whose range of meaning is well suited to this purpose. But he cannot have hoped or intended that the Greek-speaking community for whom the Septuagint was produced would understand him to be specifying laughter. The use of *sugchairo* at Genesis 21:6 does not alter the fact that it is not a verb for 'laugh'. Stibbe says that it 'means *literally* to rejoice with someone'[20] which carries the implication that it is commonly used non-literally to mean 'laugh with'; but this is not the case.

The same principle applies to Psalm 126:2, which Stibbe also uses in his attempt to develop the idea that *sugchairo* means joyful laughter. English translations of this verse contain a reference to laughter: '... then our mouths were filled with laughter (= Heb. *sechoq*)' (NIV). The Septuagint, however, renders the Hebrew word *sechoq* as *chara* (joy). Pointing to the link between *sugchairo* and *chara,* Stibbe offers this as an example of his *sugchairo* category of laughter. But it must be clearly understood that the Septuagint is rendering the *general sense* of Psalm 126:2 by employing a word which does not denote laughter. *Chara* is no more a word for 'laughter' than *sugchairo* is a word for 'laugh'.

However, having equated *sugchairo* with laughter, Stibbe goes on to ascribe significance to occurrences of the verb in the New Testament. It is true that he does not actually state that these occurrences denote laughter; but he says that 'it is interesting to note that the same word is used by Luke' in 1:58, 15:6 and 15:9.[21] This is calculated to suggest that an aura of laughter clings to *sugchairo* because it is used in the Septuagint of Genesis 21:6; although, as we have seen, the notion of laughter is simply not present in the verb's range of meaning. These New Testament references function so as to partially conceal something that might seem to present a problem: the fact that, on Stibbe's terms, the New Testament contains no references at all to joyful laughter. (The three occurrences of *katagelao* — Matthew 9:24; Mark 5:40; Luke 8:53 — are obviously derisive. Luke

[20] *Refreshing,* p. 117; my italics.

[21] Other occurrences of *sugchairo* in the New Testament are 1 Corinthians 12:26 and 13:6; Philippians 2:17,18.

6:21, 25 and James 4:9 all contain *gelao* / *gelos* and so, on Stibbe's terms, must automatically be derisive.)

This process of categorizing and labelling types of laughter is the sole use which Stibbe makes of the 31 Old Testament references in his list. The process is not linguistically legitimate and thus Stibbe fails to show that these references contribute towards the construction of a biblical case. No attempt is made to demonstrate that the references authenticate the current phenomenon of laughter by assuring us that God commends, approves or sanctions it. Of the six New Testament verses, three are not discussed at all (Matt. 9:24; Mk. 5:40; Lk. 8:53) and one (Lk. 6:25) receives a passing reference. Of James 4:9 Stibbe notes that it prohibits a certain type of laughter.

Luke 6:21 is the only reference considered in any detail. I will now evaluate all 37 verses adduced by Stibbe, as regards their ability to provide biblical support for the unusual phenomenon of laughter.[22]

(3) Evaluation

A sound case for maintaining that ecstatic laughter of the type associated with the Blessing is 'biblical' would need to demonstrate two things: firstly, that the passages referred to might properly be regarded as addressed to Christians by way of either command or exhortation; secondly, that the laughter referred to might properly be equated with the 'extraordinary phenomenon' of laughter which we are considering. (Laughter *per se* is *not* an extraordinary phenomenon.) This equation must take account of those characteristics which actually constitute the 'extraordinary phenomenon' of ecstatic laughter.

In fact it is not possible to construct a biblical case in support of the phenomenon from Stibbe's list of references. The 'extraordinary phenomenon' of laughter is laughter which:

---

[22] In Genesis 38:23, Job 22:19b and Psalm 80:6, the idea of laughter as such is not present in the Hebrew text. The noun *buz* (Gen. 38:23) and the verb *la*^{c}*ag* (Job 22:19b, Ps. 80:6) connote 'contempt' and 'to mock, deride, scorn' respectively, but not laughter (cf. Appendix B). However, I will deal with these in terms of the English translations in Stibbe's list.

a) is uncontrolled/uncontrollable
b) is prolonged beyond a usual duration
c) occurs in the absence of the usual stimuli of laughter[23]
d) is believed to be a specifically religious experience due to the unmediated activity of the Holy Spirit[24]
e) usually takes place in the communal context of a public meeting.

Let us consider the verses in Stibbe's list in the light of the above two criteria.

Genesis 17:17, 18:12, 18:13 and 18:15 refer to the sceptically mocking laughter with which Abraham and Sarah responded to God's promise concerning the birth of Isaac; this clearly cannot be a model for Christian behaviour. The same may be said of *Genesis 38:23* and 2 *Chronicles 30:10*. The former concerns the contemptuous laughter of which Judah fears he may become the object as a result of his relationship with a prostitute; the latter refers to the mocking laughter with which Israel refused the summons to Hezekiah's Passover. *Job 5:22, 8:21 and 22:19* might in isolation appear to be promises to the righteous. However, they are in fact the advice given to Job by Eliphaz and Bildad, men whom God denounces as those 'who have not spoken of me what is right' (Job 42:7).

Job 39:18 refers to the ostrich; *Job 39:22* to the horse; and *Job 4:29* to leviathan. Lest any should suppose that their examples are none the less relevant, the context shows that they are not held up as patterns to follow but as instances of the mysteries of creation beyond Job's comprehension.

Psalms 2:4, 37:13 and 59:8 describe the derisive laughter of God against his enemies. It is scarcely safe to assume without good cause that what is appropriate to God is appropriate to his people. We may include in this category *Proverbs 1:26* (where Wisdom laughs at the calamity of the wicked) on the view that Wisdom here represents the prophetic voice of God.

In *Psalm 80:6, Lamentations 1:7, Ezekiel* 23:32 and *Habakkuk 1:10*, Israel's enemies laugh at her; *Matthew 9:24, Mark 5:40* and *Luke*

---

[23] Concerning characteristics a)—c), cf. the accounts of Anne Pringle's and Tim Fordham's experiences: *Refreshing*, pp. 121 and 136 respectively.

[24] *Refreshing*, pp. 124, 128.

8:53 describe the scornful laughter with which the mourners greeted Jesus at the home of Jairus; and *Luke 6:25* concerns those of whom Jesus said, 'Woe to you that laugh now . . .' and whose present laughter will ultimately be turned to weeping. Again, none of these can be viewed as models for Christian experience. The same is also true of *Proverbs 29:9* and *Ecclesiastes 7:6*, which concern the laughter of fools (unless we take them as warnings). *Psalm 52:6* refers to the righteous laughing at the downfall of the wicked. The application of this to Christian experience strikes me as extremely problematic; I will return to this in connection with Stibbe's interpretation of Luke 6:21. At this point I would draw attention to the fact that attitudes to enemies and evildoers under the Old Covenant were specifically challenged by Jesus himself in Matthew 5:38–48; and that Galatians 6:10 enjoins us to do good to all, especially (and therefore not exclusively) to believers. And how is the task of evangelism to be reconciled with rejoicing at the downfall of the wicked?

Thus all these verses fail to satisfy the first criterion: they do not speak to Christians concerning their experience and behaviour. It is scarcely necessary to point out that in any case the laughter they describe cannot be equated with the unusual phenomenon of ecstatic laughter.

Proverbs 14:13 and *Ecclesiastes 2:2*, *3:4*, *7:3* and *10:19* are general philosophical reflections on laughter and the human condition. I do not deny that Christians may study these reflections with profit, but they will not find in them encouragement to laugh nor any mention of the sort of laughter associated with the Toronto blessing. The industrious wife of *Proverbs 31:25* may be considered an admirable role model (or not, according to one's point of view); either way, her laughter ('she laughs at the time to come') must be taken non-literally, a consideration which might be urged in a number of the above cases, though I will not insist on it.

Stibbe makes use of *Genesis 21:6* and *Psalm 126:2* in formulating his definitions but nowhere explains how these verses relate to Christian experience. The former records Sarah's laughter and predicts that of her neighbours at the birth of Isaac; the latter describes the laughter of the freed captives returning to Zion. Since these passages do not directly address the issue of laughter but merely record instances of it, the question arises of what may be legitimately inferred. Certainly nothing in either text condemns the laughter; but neither is there anything to indicate that it was expected or required. The most that can be concluded is that the Bible does not forbid laughter as an expression of joyful gratitude to God. But what sort of laughter? It is not possible to equate the laughter in these verses with the 'unusual phenomenon' under discussion. Neither text describes uncontrolled or unusually prolonged laughter. It was not mysterious or inexplicable in normal terms; if questioned, those who laughed could have pointed to a specific and normal reason for their laughter. Nor does the text say that they laughed as a result of being acted on directly by the Holy Spirit; they laughed for joy at the deliverance God had wrought in external circumstances, not because they had had an unmediated spiritual experience of God.[25]

We are left with *James 4:9* and *Luke 6:21*, the only two verses which address Christians directly and explicitly on the subject of laughter. The former rebukes the careless laughter which shows the absence of humility and repentance; this need not here concern us. Luke 6:21, then, is the only verse in the Bible which positively and specifically predicates laughter of Christians. It does not speak of uncontrolled, prolonged, unusual laughter of the sort to be observed currently. In fact, it does not speak of laughter in the present at all, but of laughter in the future. It is the laughter of those who have come into possession of the kingdom of God (Luke 6:20) and of their heavenly reward (Luke 6:23).

This means that it is difficult — even impossible — to accept Stibbe's view that the laughter is derisive. This view is in fact based solely on his assumption concerning *gelao*, which assumption, we have seen, results from a faulty methodology. If we come to Luke 6:21 without faulty assumptions we have no reason to suppose that the laughter is derisive. The language used does not define the type of laughter, which must therefore be deduced from the wider context. Since this passage speaks of the final condition of the people of God and of the blessing and heavenly reward which they will enjoy in his kingdom, it is from

[25] I do not propose to examine those additional occurrences in the Septuagint of verbs for 'laugh' (not mentioned in Stibbe's list) which I mentioned above. The references are noted in Appendix A; anyone who cares to examine them will find that they fail to satisfy the two criteria I have set out.

this that the quality of the laughter must be inferred. Can we suppose that the blessed condition of sharing in the joy of the kingdom will consist for Christians in mocking those among whom they would themselves have been numbered except for the grace of God? We must conclude that Jesus is promising laughter purely of rejoicing in his presence.

This laughter, as I have said, is explicitly reserved for the future, for the kingdom of God. Stibbe's use of this verse to authenticate the current phenomenon assumes that Christians are currently experiencing an anticipation of the eschatological laughter of Luke 6:21: 'As the world's last night draws near the disciples of Jesus will find the scornful laughter of victory and superiority beginning to flow from their mouths.'[26]

I have already argued that the laughter promised by Jesus cannot be derisive and must be joyful. But furthermore, it is important to note that Luke 6:21 itself says simply, 'You will laugh', referring to the future joy of the kingdom. There is no suggestion here that we may expect to have in the present any experience of laughter which constitutes an anticipation of this eschatological reality — let alone one such as that associated with the Toronto blessing. Nor does the Bible anywhere even hint at such a possibility. The New Testament does indeed say that Christians may have in the present a foretaste of the joy of heaven; though they do not yet see Christ, they believe in him 'and are filled with an inexpressible and glorious joy' (I Pet 1:8, NIV). But that we may expect this to be accompanied by the unusual phenomenon of prolonged, uncontrolled laughter cannot be maintained from the Bible.

I have sought to demonstrate that Stibbe fails to construct a convincing case from the biblical material which he has adduced, and that such a case cannot in fact be made. However, some advocates of the Toronto blessing would argue (though Stibbe does not) that the authentication of unusual phenomena does not depend on the construction of a positive biblical case. It will be helpful to examine the method by which they seek to legitimate the phenomena. This method is the 'test book' method. I believe it represents an unsound approach to the authority of Scripture.

---

[26] *Refreshing*, p. 129.

3. 'Not a *Text* Book but a *Test* Book'

In countering arguments that unusual phenomena such as ecstatic laughter are not biblical, supporters of the Toronto blessing often reply that 'the Bible is not a text book, but a test book'. This assertion is usually made in conjunction with the claim that we cannot expect to find a biblical reference for everything we do as Christians and that the absence of such a reference cannot be held to invalidate a particular practice. If the statement that the Bible is not a text book were made in any other context, it might be understood as meaning that, while the Bible contains a great deal of information concerning what is sound Christian practice, it does not offer ready-made answers to each and every particular question we might be asking. That is, we might have to make comparisons, draw deductions etc., in order to obtain an answer. Most Christians would probably agree with this, but the second element in the sentence suggests that something rather different is in mind. To say that the Bible is '**not** a text book **but** a test book', places the two descriptions in opposition to each other; the sentence speaks of two different things. The Bible is *not* one sort of thing *but* another. How are we to understand this? If we take the words seriously, they are telling us that the Bible is *not* any longer to be regarded as an authoritative source of information concerning Christian practice, *but* only as a device for testing the validity of information derived from some (unspecified) source. If pursued to its logical conclusion, such a view opens up the possibility of a church constantly engaged in testing an agenda of Christian practice drawn from who-knows-where, rather than taking Scripture as a starting point. Depending on the effectiveness of the testing, this procedure would prove at best very time-wasting and at worst, disastrous.

(1) Scriptural, Unscriptural and Non-Scriptural

Sometimes, the claim that the Bible is not a text book but a test book is made in conjunction with a threefold distinction between scriptural, unscriptural and non-scriptural (or biblical, unbiblical and non-biblical). We find this approach in an article by

Gerald Coates ('Toronto and Scripture', *Renewal* 222, Nov, 1994), though he is not alone in adopting the method.[27]

Coates distinguishes between things which God specifically approves of (these are 'scriptural'); things which God specifically disapproves of (these are 'unscriptural'); and things which fall into neither of these categories (these are 'plainly non-scriptural'). He then says that 'the Bible is not a text book but a test book. We draw our experiences alongside scripture to test them to see whether they are of God or not'. It is natural to ask how are we to proceed if, when we do this, we discover that God neither specifically approves nor specifically disapproves? According to Coates, in such cases 'we are given liberty to develop a wide range of activities' which 'broadly reflect' things God approves of. Things approved in this category include Sunday schools, youth groups and 'quiet times'.

Coates points out that in the exercise of our 'liberty to develop a wide range of activities', we have accepted Sunday schools etc., and goes on to suggest we should therefore accept that 'the same liberty applies to manifestations of the Holy Spirit's presence'.

On examination, this parallel turns out to be not simply incomplete, but fatally flawed.

(2) A Flawed Parallel

One obvious weakness in Coates's argument is the difference between, for example, Sunday school and the manifestations associated with the Toronto blessing. The Sunday school is an institution of human devising and Sunday school work is an activity in which people engage of their own volition and which is under their own control. Physical manifestations, on the other hand, are understood to be experiences which come from outside the person affected, are not of human devising nor under the subject's control, but have their origin in the will and activity

[27] Early in 1995, in a letter 'responding to questions regarding some of the phenomena experienced in recent Vineyard meetings' John Wimber places the phenomenon of animal noises into the category of 'non-biblical'. In October 1995 I attended a meeting at St Thomas' Church, Crookes, Sheffield, which was hosted by the Rector Mike Breen, to whom Stibbe refers in *Times of Refreshing*. At this meeting an approach similar to that adopted by Coates was endorsed.

of God himself. They are, in Coates's words, 'a response to the Holy Spirit's presence'. If this were indeed the case, it is difficult to see what it has to do with our 'liberty to develop a wide range of activities'. Surely we cannot exercise discretion as to whether we will or will not respond to the presence of the Holy Spirit? And is it really appropriate to speak of God's direct actions, or the results of those actions, as doing no more than 'broadly reflect[ing]' things he approves of? This would appear to introduce into our concept of God notions of uncertainty and inconsistency. Does Coates really mean that God neither specifically approves nor specifically disapproves of his own direct actions and their results?

Another weakness appears when we begin to consider the relationship between Sunday schools or the Toronto Blessing and God's sovereign authority. No one has ever claimed that the sovereign authority of God rests on the institution of Sunday school qua institution. Many may have urged the necessity of preaching the gospel to children and training them in godly ways, and commended Sunday schools as a means of accomplishing these ends. But no one has claimed for them the status of a sovereign move of God, whereas this is claimed for the Toronto blessing and its associated manifestations. Because Scripture does not command the institution of Sunday school, it cannot claim this status. Such activities are not binding on all Christians, and while we ourselves might accept and approve them we do so on the basis that others might not. We are not therefore committed to accepting as legitimate all other things which fall into the same category. Thus, if it is argued that 'liberty' as applied to Sunday schools is the same as 'liberty' regarding manifestations, we should be free either to accept or reject the manifestations. But in fact, advocates of the Toronto blessing are not offering this option. They insist that we accept them and refrain from criticizing them. In addition, if their claims concerning the manifestations are true, rejection and criticism are not in any case an option. The activities of the Holy Spirit are not an optional matter.

Coates's argument is not actually about our 'liberty to develop a wide range of activities'. What he is really saying is that to accept Sunday schools is to concede the principle that everything in the 'non-scriptural' category of things of which God neither specifically approves nor specifically disapproves must be regarded as legitimate.

This argument ignores an essential distinction. The claims made for the manifestations are pitched much higher than in the case of the Sunday school. The Sunday school makes no greater claim for itself than that it is an expedient method of performing certain God-given tasks. It is also provisional; we are free to abandon it if a better method occurs to us. In such a case, it is enough that we receive God's *nihil obstat*; that though there is nothing in the Bible to indicate that he approves of this particular method, there is nothing to indicate that he disapproves. But the claim in the case of the manifestations is different; here is no question of a provisional expedient but of a response to the very presence of the Holy Spirit himself. Surely it is not unreasonable to demand that such large claims produce stronger credentials than are required in the case of a provisional expedient? The magnitude of the claim should be reflected in the strength of the evidence. The greater the claim, the greater the potential for disaster if it should prove false; therefore a higher degree of certainty is most surely called for. The only sort of evidence which can bear the weight of such claims as these is evidence which assures us that God wholly approves of these phenomena.

I would argue that the attempt to legitimate unusual phenomena by reference to the category of 'non-scriptural' things is wholly inadequate. The fact that ecstatic laughter — and other, more bizarre phenomena — are not mentioned in the Bible with either approval or disapproval is simply not enough to settle the matter when the question under consideration is whether or not they can be attributed to the presence of the Holy Spirit. Before we dare assert that they can — for the reputation of God himself is at stake — we must have grounds much more positive than this.

If the Bible is to be used as a test book, the stringency of the testing procedure must be adequate to the issue involved. But more than this, we must not use the Bible *only* as a test book. We must use it also as a 'text book' in the sense of an authoritative source; we must *begin* with the Bible. Adherence to this principle is another ingredient in the superior claim to legitimacy of the Sunday school, as against the phenomena associated with the Toronto blessing. Those who instituted Sunday schools based their agenda on the commands of the Bible and devised a method of fulfilling these commands; and since the Bible offers no objection to such a method they were justified in adopting it. It appears that the first item in this sequence has been omitted in the case of the Toronto blessing. Its defenders are engaged in testing an agenda; but had the Bible been the starting point, it is doubtful whether such an agenda would have suggested itself. And the vocabulary used in describing the test procedure reduces the question to one of whether God approves or disapproves of what we are doing. This suggests that the initiative in formulating the agenda lies with us, whereas in fact, in the Bible, God has set an agenda for us. He wants the first word as well as the last.

Bibliography

Edwards, J., 'A Narrative of Surprising Conversions' in *Jonathan Edwards on Revival* (London: Banner of Truth, 1994)

—, 'The Distinguishing Marks of a Work of the Spirit of God' in *Jonathan Edwards on Revival* (London: Banner of Truth, 1994)

—, 'Some Thoughts Concerning the Present Revival of Religion in New England', in *The Works of Jonathan Edwards,* Vol 1 (London: Banner of Truth, 1992)

Gunter, W. Stephen, *The Limits of Love Divine, John Wesley's Response to Antinomianism and Enthusiasm* (Kingswood: Nashville, 1989)

Nida, E., 'Implications of Contemporary Linguistics for Biblical Scholarship', *JBL* 91 (1972)

Stibbe, M., *Times of Refreshing: A Practical Theology of Revival for Today* (London: Marshall Pickering, 1995)

Appendix A

Greek Words for Laugh/Laughter in the New Testament

gelao (v)	katagelao (v)	gelos (n)
Luke 6:21	Matt. 9:24	Jas. 4:9
Luke 6:25	Mark 5:40	
	Luke 8:53	

Greek Words for Laugh/Laughter used in the Septuagint: Stibbe's List

(Chapter and verse references are to English versions; n = noun, v = verb)

<u>Derisive</u>

gelao (v)	gelos (n)	katagelao (v)	ekgelao (v)	epigelao (v)	mukterizo (v)*	empaizo (v)*	euphraino (v)*
Gen. 17:17	Ezek. 23:32	Gen. 38:23	Ps. 2:4	Prov. 1:26	Job 22:19	Hab. 1:10 (c)	Prov. 31:25
Gen. 18:12		2Chr. 30:10	Ps. 37:13		Ps. 80:6		
Gen. 18:13		Job 5:22	Ps. 59:18				
Gen. 18:15 (×2)		Job 39:18					
Ps. 52:6		Job 39:22					
Lam. 1:7		Job 41:29					
		Prov. 29:9					

* See Appendix B.

Non-Derisive

gelao (v)	gelos (n)		sugchairo (v)	chara (n)	euphrosune (n)
Eccles. 3:4	Gen. 21:6(a)		Gen. 21:6 (b)	Ps. 126:2	Prov. 14:13
	Job 8:21				
	Eccles. 2:2	In these there is irony on the part of the *speaker;* i.e. he is making ironic			
	Eccles. 7:3	statements *about* laughter but nothing suggests that the laughter about which			
	Eccles. 10:19	he is speaking is ironic or mocking.			
	Eccles. 7:6	The laughter of a fool is certainly foolish laughter, but this is not at all the same as derisive laughter.			

Greek Verbs for Laugh Elsewhere in the Septuagint (Canonical Books Only)

Derisive:	gelao	katagelao	ekgelao
	Job 22:19	Job 9:23	Neh. 2:19
		Job 21:3	Neh. 4:1
		Job 30:1	
		Job 39:7	
		Ps. 25:2	
		Prov. 17:5	
		Prov. 30:17	
		Mic. 3:7	

Non-Derisive:	gelao
	Job 29:24

Gelao also occurs in Job 19:7 (some manuscripts) and in Jer. 20:8; identification between the Septuagint and the Hebrew text from which our English translations were made is doubtful and the use of gelao is obscure.

Appendix B

I have said that *mukterizo, empaizo and euphraino* do not denote laughter as such. Why then does the word 'laugh' appear in some English translations of the verses in which these terms occur? To answer this question we need to take account of the Hebrew text of which both the Septuagint and our English Bibles are translations.

In the case of Habakkuk 1:10c) (*empaizo*) and Proverbs 31:25 (*euphraino*) the verb used in the Hebrew text is *sachaq*, which includes in its range of meaning: to laugh (simply); to laugh at (derisively); to scorn, deride. In Habakkuk 1:10, therefore, some English translations have chosen to render *sachaq* by 'laugh at' (NIV); others have chosen 'despise' (NEB) or 'deride' (AV). The Septuagint translators, in choosing *empaizo* — to trifle with, to mock — did something similar to NEB and AV — i.e., they chose a verb which connotes derision but not laughter.

In Proverbs 31:25, NEB and NIV have chosen to render *sachaq* by 'can afford to laugh at' and 'can laugh at' respectively, inclining to the 'laugh at (derisively)' connotation; AV, inclining to the 'laugh (simply)' meaning of *sachaq* has rendered it 'rejoice'. The Septuagint translators adopted an approach similar to that of AV; that is, they chose *euphraino* — to make merry, to rejoice, with no suggestion of actual laughter. (Incidentally, of course, this means that while in some English translations, including Stibbe's, this verse falls into the 'derisive' category it does not do so in the Septuagint.)

The range of meaning of *mukterizo* is 'to sneer, to mock, to deride' — a range which corresponds quite closely to that of the Hebrew verb (*la*^{c}*ag*) which it translates in Job 22:19 b) and Psalm 80:6, NIV, for example, translates *la*^{c}*ag* by 'mock' in both instances. AV on the other hand has 'laugh to scorn' and 'laugh among themselves'; these quite properly render the sense of the text into English and this is a perfectly legitimate translation technique. But it is not a guide to the way in which *mukterizo* functions within its own language system; study of the semantic values of words should always be monolingual.

Appendix C

STIBBE'S LIST OF REFERENCES

Genesis 17:17	Then Abraham fell on his face and laughed, and said to himself, 'Shall a child be born to a man who is a hundred years old? Shall Sarah, who is ninety years old, bear a child?'
Genesis 18:12	So Sarah laughed to herself saying, 'After I have grown old, and my husband is old, shall I have pleasure?'
Genesis 18:13	The LORD said to Abraham, 'Why did Sarah laugh and say "Shall I indeed bear a child, now that I am old?" '
Genesis 18:15	But Sarah denied, saying 'I did not laugh'; for she was afraid. He said, 'No, but you did laugh'.
Genesis 21:6	And Sarah said, 'God has made laughter for me; everyone who hears will laugh over me'.[1]
Genesis 38:23	And Judah replied, 'Let her keep the things as her own, lest we be laughed at'.
2 Chronicles 30:10	So the couriers went from city to city through the country of E'phraim and

[1] This translation is taken from RSV, which has a derisive nuance in the second reference to laughter. However, in discussing the verse on page 116 of *Times of Refreshing*, Stibbe uses NIV: ' . . . everyone who hears about this will laugh with me'. I have therefore placed Genesis 21:6 in the non-derisive category in Appendix A.

	Manasseh, and as far as Zeb'ulun; but they laughed them to scorn and mocked them.
Job 5:22	At destruction and famine you shall laugh, and shall not fear the beasts of the earth.
Job 8:21	He will fill your mouth with laughter, and your lips with shouting.
Job 22:19	The righteous see it and are glad; the innocent laugh them to scorn.
Job 39:18	When she rouses herself to flee, she laughs at the horse and his rider.
Job 39:22	He laughs at fear, and is not dismayed; he does not turn back from the sword.
Job 41:29	Clubs are counted as stubble; he laughs at the rattle of javelins.
Psalm 2:4	He who sits in the heaven laughs; the LORD has them in derision.
Psalm 37:13	But the LORD laughs at the wicked, for he sees that his day is coming.
Psalm 52:6	The righteous shall see, and fear, and shall laugh at him . . .
Psalm 59:8	But thou, O LORD, dost laugh at them; thou dost hold the nations in derision.
Psalm 80:6	Thou dost make us the scorn of our neighbours and our enemies laugh among themselves.
Psalm 126:2	Then our mouth was filled with laughter, and our tongue with shouts of joy.
Proverbs 1:26	I also will laugh at your calamity; I will mock them when panic strikes you.
Proverbs 14:13	Even in laughter the heart is sad, and the end of joy is grief.
Proverbs 29:9	If a wise man has an argument with a fool, the fool only rages and laughs, and there is no quiet.
Proverbs 31:25	Strength and dignity are her clothing, and she laughs at the time to come.
Ecclesiastes 2:2	I said of laughter, 'It is mad'.
Ecclesiastes 3:4	A time to weep and a time to laugh . . .
Ecclesiastes 7:3	Sorrow is better than laughter.

Ecclesiastes 7:6	For as the crackling of thorns under a pot, so is the laughter of the fool; this also is vanity.
Ecclesiastes 10:19	Bread is made for laughter, and wine gladdens life, and money answers everything.
Lamentations 1:7	Her enemies looked at her and laughed at her destruction.
Ezekiel 23:32	Thus says the LORD God: 'You shall drink your sister's cup which is deep and large; you shall be laughed at and held in derision, for it contains much.'
Habakkuk 1:10	At kings they scoff, and of rulers they make sport. They laugh at every fortress, for they heap up earth and take it.
Matthew 9:24	He said, 'Depart; for the girl is not dead but sleeping.' And they laughed at him.
Mark 5:40	And they laughed at him.
Luke 6:21	Blessed are you that weep now, for you shall laugh.
Luke 6:25	Woe to you that laugh now, for you shall mourn and weep.
Luke 8:53	And they laughed at him.
James 4:9	Be wretched and mourn and weep. Let your laughter be turned to mourning and your joy to dejection.

Chapter 4
The Gamaliel Principle

1. 'Wait and See'

Many people have reacted to the 'Blessing' uncritically, either denouncing it as satanic, professing indifference or embracing it completely and enthusiastically. But others have adopted more critical approaches and have attempted to justify their own responses to the 'Blessing' by biblical means. One example is the response of the Salvation Army in the UK, quoted by Dave Roberts.[1] 'As the autumn [of 1994] approached, [the UK leader of the Salvation Army] Commissioner Pender, encouraged corps around the country to observe the Gamaliel principle — [namely] if it was not of God, it would come to nothing; if it was God at work, it would be foolish to oppose him!'[2]

This argument is often being used by those who approve of the 'Blessing'. They quote the words of the Pharisee Gamaliel, when he spoke about the refusal of Peter and John to obey the Jewish leaders and stop proclaiming the good news about Jesus: 'Leave these men alone! For if their purpose or activity is of human origin, it will fail. But if it is from God, you will not be able to stop these men; you will only find yourselves fighting against God.' In Pender's case this principle is, it seems, being used in order to advise Christians to engage in the 'Blessing' without worrying too much about its origins.

A further use of the principle by Toronto proponents can be found in the work of Mark Stibbe. Responding to letters about his exegesis of Ezekiel 47 (see chapter 2 above), he writes:

---

1 *The 'Toronto Blessing'*.

2 Ibid. p. 37.

> I am extremely grateful . . . Many of their criticisms are justified, though I do disagree profoundly with Jo Gardner's view of the current move of the Spirit. [Gardner views the Toronto Blessing as demonic.] That seems to me to be a dangerous perspective to be taking and I would urge Jo and those taking a similarly dismissive line to employ the Gamaliel principle outlined in Acts 5:34ff.[3]

The reason why Stibbe urges this can be seen in *Times of Refreshing*; a book which he concludes with a discussion of blasphemy against the Holy Spirit. There he writes:

> It needs to be said here that those of a conservative evangelical or of an institutional mind-set need to be very careful not to blaspheme against the Holy Spirit [in the sense understood by Mark and Matthew — according to Stibbe, calling the work of the Holy Spirit demonic] when they speak about the Toronto Blessing. A much more Godly response from the sceptics would be that of Gamaliel in Acts 5:38 . . . . If you are a sceptic, I respectfully counsel you to take this line.[4]

These two responses (or variations on them) have been quoted incessantly by the proponents of the Toronto Blessing, who seem convinced that such responses are 'godly'. But it would be wrong to think that this positive use of Acts 5 has gone unchallenged; both Peter Masters and Tom Smail (in passing) have opposed in print the basing of an adequate Christian response upon Gamaliel's principle.[5] However, neither of them has tackled what seem to me the most important questions: (i) why the Gamaliel principle is proving so attractive to proponents of the Toronto Blessing, and (ii) why it finds such easy access into the churches which are involved.

Any attempt to answer these questions must begin by noting that this positive appraisal of Gamaliel has been around for a

---

[3] 'Four Waves of the Spirit', p. 8.

[4] *Refreshing*, p. 177.

[5] P. Masters, 'Beware of the Counsel of Gamaliel', pp. 11–13; T. Smail, 'Why My Name is Not Gamaliel', p. 8.

long time. The following two examples illustrate how the principle has been used within the Charismatic Movement apart from the Toronto Blessing. The first is contained in a popular book on discipleship by David Watson.[6] In a chapter on spiritual warfare he writes:

> John tells us in his First Letter that we are to test the spirits to see whether they are of God, and this is particularly important in an age when the cults and sects are proliferating; but this should be done with exquisite caution, lest a genuine work of God is written off as spurious, heretical or even demonic. Some have done just that with the whole of the charismatic movement, good and bad together; but they would have been wiser to have exercised the caution of Gamaliel, for 'if it is of God . . . you might even be found opposing God!'[7]

The second example comes from a recent book about house church leaders entitled *Doing a New Thing*.[8] John Noble describes his fellowship's experience of being ostracized in the early 1970s; 'The only person who publicly defended us was Brian Richardson from the Elim movement. He wisely took the Gamaliel approach, that if what we were doing was of God, it would prosper . . . we were encouraged by his refusal to jump on the bandwagon of criticism that was hitting us from every direction.'[9]

In these examples we again have a positive use of Gamaliel and his principle. But this positive appraisal has by no means been limited to charismatics. Many commentators on Acts describe Gamaliel's words as 'wiser counsel'[10] or as 'good advice'.[11] Theodore Ferris regards Gamaliel as a 'perfect instance of the moderating influence of the judicial mind', and his counsel

6 *Discipleship*.
7 Ibid. pp. 171–2.
8 B. Hewitt, 'John Noble', in *Doing a New Thing*, pp. 177–97.
9 Ibid. p. 184.
10 D.J. Williams, *Acts*, NIBC, p. 111.
11 G.A. Krodel, *Acts*. Augsburg Commentary, p. 129.

as one of 'wise restraint'.[12] One can also find a positive use of Gamaliel's words in the devotional literature. In *New Daylight: Daily readings from the Bible*, Rosemary Green writes:

> Gamaliel knew that God was sovereign and that his good purposes would be worked out. His argument was simple. 'Wait and see what happens. If this is just a human revolt it will fade, as the others did. If it is of God' — as Gamaliel probably believed — 'we do not want to be on the wrong side'. What wise words for precaution against panic reactions![13]

However, at the same time, there have also been negative verdicts on Gamaliel's principle. According to John Stott, for example:

> We should not be too ready to credit Gamaliel with having uttered an invariable principle. To be sure, in the long run what is from God will triumph and what is merely human (let alone diabolical) will not. Nevertheless, in the shorter run evil plans sometimes succeed, while good ones conceived in accordance with the will of God sometimes fail. So the Gamaliel principle is not a reliable index as to what is from God and what is not.[14]

In fact, as we shall see, these positive and negative appreciations of Gamaliel and his words have a very long history which takes in many church traditions.

---

[12] *Acts*. Interpreter's Bible Commentary, p. 86. Many liberal Christians seem to have this affinity for Gamaliel. Masters mentions an appeal to Gamaliel by the liberal theologian Harry Emerson Fosdick: 'In an infamous sermon of 1922 (entitled, 'Shall the Fundamentalists Win?'), Gamaliel is extolled as the personification of tolerance and magnanimity. Fundamentalists are urged to abandon their narrow and cantankerous unreasonableness, and to adopt the great Gamaliel's intellectual liberalism' (op. cit. p. 11). Mark Smith has also brought to my attention a positive reference to Gamaliel by the nineteenth-century liberal theologian, F. Schleiermacher. In a sermon on Gamaliel (on the first Sunday after Trinity, 1832) Schleiermacher gave the Pharisee his full approval, ('A Sermon on Gamaliel', in *Sämmtliche Werke* 2, p. 300).

[13] May–August 1993 (Bible Reading Fellowship, Oxford), p. 56. See also her similar but shortened comments in *The Church of England Newspaper* (Friday September 22, 1995), p. 12.

[14] *Acts*. The Bible Speaks Today, p. 118.

Before taking the discussion further I had better explain my own position, before justifying it. I agree with Stott, Smail and Masters that the 'Gamaliel principle' is untrue in its context in Acts — i.e. as Gamaliel uses it there. I also believe that this principle should play no part in Christian thought, especially in any attempt to formulate a response to a new movement, whether it is charismatic or not. As will be seen below, my reasons for taking this stance are historical, logical, textual and theological.

This does not mean that I think it appropriate merely to dismiss Gamaliel's words, as for example, Peter Masters has done. There has to be some reason why Christians down the centuries have viewed Gamaliel positively. Theologians have used his 'principle' openly and honestly and thus encouraged us to do so now. Indeed, Dave Roberts, in his book on the 'Blessing', quotes Jonathan Edwards as doing so. We need to understand the attraction of Gamaliel and his principle if we are to make any progress towards agreeing about what part the principle should play in Christian thinking. The purpose of what follows is to explain why Christians have such a positive image of Gamaliel and to show that this is actually an illusion which may lead to error. Although I criticize the way Gamaliel's principle is being used today, I sincerely hope that all who believe in the truth will see that this is an attempt to discuss and clarify that truth and so will be ready to respond to, and engage with, my reasoning.

In Section 2 we shall examine the ways in which Gamaliel has been understood by Jews and Christians over the centuries. We shall see that while the positive appreciation of Gamaliel by Christians has very deep historical roots, those roots are firmly located in the apparent ambiguity of Acts 5 itself. Section 3 surveys the way in which Origen, Luther, and Jonathan Edwards each made positive use of Gamaliel. The aim here is to draw out some of the historical, logical, and theological problems implicit in their use of the Gamaliel principle. Section 4 returns to the apparent textual ambiguities of Acts 5, and shows that the positive image of Gamaliel's principle projected by these ambiguities is not only an illusion, albeit an attractive one, but also one which is in conflict with Luke's own portrayal of the growth of the Christian movement. Section 5 develops a more systematic theological argument against the Gamaliel principle, building upon the problems uncovered in sections 3 and 4; it argues that Gamaliel's principle is in effect a distortion of a properly Christian view of divine providence, so that on the basis of this distorted view many Christians are saddling themselves with a response to the Toronto Blessing which is not simply inadequate but rather useless and, possibly, contrary to God's will.

2. Gamaliel: His 'Twin Careers'

In the Jewish tradition, Gamaliel the Elder is credited with certain liberal reforms in marriage, divorce, and Sabbath law.[15] However, it would be a mistake to think of this Gamaliel as an ordinary, if rather liberal, rabbi. Almost all the commentaries quote the following passage from the Mishnah: 'Since Rabban Gamaliel died there has been no more reverence for the Law, and purity and abstinence died out at the same time'.[16]

Two things are noteworthy here: Firstly, Rabban is an Aramaic term meaning 'our teacher' which was applied as an honorary title to certain distinguished men, marking them off from the more ordinary rabbi, 'my teacher'; Gamaliel the Elder was the first of only seven so-called. Secondly, Bruce Chilton has argued that since the interpretation of the Torah, the keeping of purity, and the maintenance of dietary laws were 'programmatically typical of pharisaism', Gamaliel appears to be a paradigmatic figure of that movement.[17] As F.F. Bruce has put it, he is 'the embodiment of pure pharisaism'.[18]

With this Jewish understanding of Gamaliel as the perfect Pharisee in mind it may come as a shock to realize that Gamaliel had a second career in the Christian tradition in which he played

---

[15] Gamaliel the Elder was so-called by the writers of the Mishnah in order to prevent a confusion with Gamaliel II, cf. E. Schürer. *The History of the Jewish People in the Age of Jesus Christ*, p. 368.

[16] Mishnah, *sota*, 9.15

[17] 'Gamaliel', in *Anchor Bible Dictionary*, pp. 904–6, see p. 905.

[18] *Acts of the Apostles*, NICNT, p. 115.

other roles: those of closet Christian, spy, and venerated saint. The process of transformation began early; this passage from the Clementine Recognitions dates from at least the beginning of the third century CE. The Recognitions[19] is an apocryphal tale in which Clement of Rome travels to Jerusalem in the thirties CE seeking knowledge of God. He becomes involved in a debate between the disciples and Caiaphas the high priest. Finally, Clement and Caiaphas argue.

> When I [that is Clement] had thus spoken, the whole multitude of the priests were in a rage, because I had foretold to them the overthrow of the Temple. When Gamaliel, a chief of the people, saw — who was secretly our brother in the faith, but by our advice remained among them — [that] they were greatly enraged and moved with intense fury against us, he stood up and said, 'Be quiet for a little, O men of Israel, for you do not perceive the trial which hangs over you. Wherefore refrain from these men; and if what they are engaged in be of human counsel, it will soon come to an end; but if it be from God, why will you sin without cause, and prevail nothing ? For who can overpower the will of God? Now therefore, since the day is declining towards evening, I shall myself dispute with these men tomorrow, in this same place, in your hearing, so that I may openly oppose and clearly refute every error.' By this speech of his their fury was to some extent checked, especially in the hope that next day we should be publicly convicted of error; and so he dismissed the people peacefully.[20]

The next day, Clement continues:

> . . . Gamaliel, who . . . was of our faith, but who by dispensation remained amongst them, that if at any time they should attempt anything unjust or wicked against us, he might either check them by skilfully adopted counsel,

---

19 'The Clementine Recognitions' in *Tatian, Theophilus, and the Clementine Recognitions*, pp. 179–90.
20 Ibid. p. 185.

> or might warn us, that we might either be on our guard or might turn it aside; — he therefore, as if acting against us, first of all looking to James the bishop, addressed him in this manner.[21]

However, the discussion is interrupted; the troublemaker Saul arrives, and the Christians are forced to flee the roused crowd. Later, however: '. . . one of the brethren came to us from Gamaliel . . . bringing us secret tidings that the enemy [that is Saul/Paul] had received a commission from Caiaphas...that he should arrest all who believed in Jesus, and should go to Damascus with all his letters, and that there also, employing the help of the unbelievers, he should make havoc among the faithful'.[22]

In this story Gamaliel is a Christian who is allowed to hide his faith in order to remain a member of the Sanhedrin and so help the early church avoid persecution.

This next passage comes from the homilies of the great preacher, John Chrysostom (354–407), who was Bishop of Constantinople from 398. Of all writers in Greek, Chrysostom has the most references to Gamaliel. Of 41 references in Greek texts in the millenium following the birth of Christ, 23 are by Chrysostom. Commenting on Acts 5:34, he states in his fourteenth homily:

> This Gamaliel was Paul's teacher. And one may well wonder how, being so right-minded in his judgement, and withal learned in the law, he did not yet believe. But it cannot be that he should have continued in unbelief to the end. Indeed it appears plainly from the words he here speaks. . . .Observe how judiciously he frames his speech, and how he immediately at the very outset puts them in fear. And that he may not be suspected of taking [the apostles'] part, he addresses [the Sanhedrin] as if he and they were of the same opinion . . .[23]

---

21 Ibid. p. 186.
22 Ibid. p. 189.
23 *Homilies on Acts and Romans*. p. 87.

A discussion of the Gamaliel principle follows; in Chrysostom's view 'the argument is unanswerable'.[24] He continues:

> [The Sanhedrin] were persuaded [by Gamaliel]. Then why, it may be asked, did [they] scourge [the apostles]? Such was the incontrovertible justness of his speech, they could not look it in the face; nevertheless, they sated their own animosity; and again they expected to terrify [the apostles] in this way. By the fact also of his saying these things not in the presence of the Apostles, he gained a hearing more than he would otherwise have done; and then the suavity of his discourse and the justness of what was said, helped to persuade them. In fact, this man all but preached the Gospel.[25]

Two final traditions may perhaps complete the Christian career of Gamaliel the Elder. In the seventh century Photius records having read in a work of Eustratius how Gamaliel was baptized, along with his son and Nicodemus, by St Peter and St John.[26] The other tradition is that Gamaliel's body was miraculously discovered in the fifth century and was preserved in Pisa, Italy, as an object of veneration.[27]

Gamaliel's twin careers are summed up in polemical Christian terms by Matthew Henry in his *Commentary:*

> The tradition of the Jewish writers is, that . . . [Gamaliel] lived and died an inveterate enemy to Christ and his Gospel; . . . [But] the tradition of the papists is that he turned Christian, and became an eminent patron of Christianity, and a follower of Paul, who . . . had [previously] sat at his feet. [However,] if that were so, it is very probable we should have heard of him somewhere in the Acts or Epistles.[28]

[24] Ibid. p. 88.
[25] Ibid. p. 88.
[26] Ibid. p. 87. See footnote 1.
[27] F.E. Gigot, 'Gamaliel', in *The Catholic Encyclopaedia*, Vol. 6, pp. 374–5; p. 375.
[28] Vol. III, p. 548.

This last conclusion has as much force now as it had in Henry's day; if Gamaliel had converted surely we would know of it — could the Rabbis have cast a Christian as the paradigmatic Pharisee? It seems to me highly unlikely that any historian would argue for the historicity of the Clementine Recognitions account and that Gamaliel was a Christian. How then do we account for his alternative career? There are, I suggest, two reasons why Gamaliel has had such a successful career as a Christian. The first is that he is one of several characters whom the early church eventually took over from the New Testament narratives, and 'christianized'. Other examples include Nicodemus, who was baptized with Gamaliel according to Photius and lent his name to a Christian work, the so-called Gospel of Nicodemus; and Pilate, who is the hero of the Acts of Pilate (which is part of the Gospel of Nicodemus), and is considered a saint in many parts of the church.

However, there is no Gospel of Caiaphas or Acts of Annas; they were impossible to christianize. There is an apparent ambiguity about Luke's portrayal of Gamaliel which enables him to be seen as positive towards Christianity. It is, I suggest, the combination of the christianizing tendency and the ambivalence of the Gamaliel of Acts 5, which seem most likely to resolve the historical conundrum of Gamaliel and his twin careers.

3. Three Historical Viewpoints and their Inherent Problems

We have noted the apparent ambivalence of Gamaliel as he appears in Acts. An appreciative view of him has been strengthened by certain Christian theologians, including Origen, Martin Luther, and Jonathan Edwards, who have appropriated his principle positively. Defining the problems which this has created will aid us when we return to the texts of Acts.

(1) Origen

Origen (185–253) was one of the greatest scholars of the early church, and perhaps the foremost exponent of the allegorical method of the Alexandrian school. Most of his works were lost following his condemnation as a heretic after his death, but one which survives, *Contra Celsus*,[29] contains a reference to Gamaliel. This is a polemical work written in response to the work of Celsus, a philosopher, who had attacked Christianity around 175. Celsus had referred to 'a Jew' who argued against the claims being made by Christians that Jesus was the fulfilment of biblical prophecies: 'But some thousands, so Celsus' Jew says, will refute Jesus by asserting that the prophecies which were applied to him were spoken of them.'[30]

Origen responded: 'We do not know whether Celsus knew of some who came to this life and wanted to emulate Jesus and to give to themselves the title of sons of God or a power of God.'[31] In the interests of truth Origen offered Celsus some examples — Theudas, Judas the Galilean, and the Samaritan Dositheus, — using the Gamaliel principle to refute their claims:

> But we may reasonably quote the very wise saying of Gamaliel in the Acts of the Apostles, to show that these men had nothing to do with the promise, and were neither sons of God nor His powers, whereas Jesus the Christ was truly God's son. Gamaliel there said: 'If this counsel or this doctrine be of men, it will be overthrown', even as theirs perished when they died; . . .[32]

He underlines this point by referring to Simon of Samaria (Acts 8):

> But now of all the [followers of Simon] in the world it is not possible, I believe, to find thirty, and perhaps I have exaggerated the number. There are very few in Palestine, while in the rest of the world he is nowhere mentioned, though his ambition was to spread his fame throughout it. Where his name is mentioned, it comes from the Acts of the Apostles, and the only people who speak of him are

---

[29] Quotations are from *Origen: Contra Celsum*, pp 52–3. Origen's comments on Gamaliel are in Book 1, section 57.

[30] Ibid. p 52.

[31] Ibid. p 52.

[32] Ibid. p 52–3.

> Christians, while the facts manifestly witnessed that there was nothing divine about Simon.[33]

There are two significant features about Origen's use of the Gamaliel principle. The first is the element of subjectivity in defining what counts as a fulfilment of the principle. According to the common understanding of Gamaliel one should know that any plan or work not from God will be overthrown. Origen can argue, more or less plausibly, for this point concerning Theudas and Dositheus (Judas I will return to shortly). But Simon still has disciples; there are not many of them, but they do exist. So Origen cannot cite Simon's lack of disciples as a criterion of the fulfilment of Gamaliel's principle as he has against the others, but rather must invoke the fact that his fame is due to Christians. Indeed the existence of some disciples, it could be argued, is a sign that Simon has not been a complete failure, particularly if one invokes the biblical concept of a remnant. The point to note is that the question of validating criteria is a problematic one which will eventually contribute to our conclusion that the principle is unworkable.

The second noteworthy feature of Origen's use of the principle concerns Judas the Galilean. This example runs into the same difficulty as that concerning Simon. According to Gamaliel (Acts 5:36, 37), this insurgent had perished, his men had been scattered, and his human work had been overthrown; Origen agrees with Gamaliel. However, as David Williams points out: 'Gamaliel speaks of [Judas'] insurrection as coming to nothing — as he could only have done at this time (around 34–5 AD), but not some ten years later, when the followers of Judas had again gathered . . . to become the zealots.'[34] According to Krodel, 'it was only after the [Jewish] war [of 66–73CE that] the zealots had become thoroughly discredited'.[35]

In the light of these comments, it is clear that Gamaliel's own example of his principle is useless. Judas the Galilean's insurrection has not come to an end when Gamaliel says it has. But Krodel (and therefore Origen) is wrong in believing that the

---

33 Ibid. p. 53.
34 *Acts*, p. 115.
35 *Acts*, p. 130.

zealots were finished after the Jewish war; firstly, because there was a second Jewish war in 132–135 under the leadership of Simon Bar-Kochba, again crushed by Rome, and secondly, because in the modern state of Israel the site of the zealot's 'finest hour', Masada, has become such a symbol of courage that one nationalistic Israeli poet was moved to write, 'Masada shall not fall again!'[36] This symbolism has also been appropriated by the armoured brigades of the Israeli Defence Forces, whose recruits take their oath of allegiance on the summit of Masada. Apparently the zealot spirit has long outlived its supposed overthrow as reported by Gamaliel.

Thus the historical evidence of the last two thousand years has contradicted Gamaliel's and Origen's use of the Gamaliel principle against Judas the Galilean. Furthermore, if we agree with both that Judas and his movement were not divine in origin, we must conclude that mere durability can be no guarantee of the God-givenness of a particular movement. Gamaliel's principle that what is not of God will be overthrown proves useless as a measure within a historical setting.

This point has also been noted by Tom Smail, with regard to the longevity of the major world religions, some of which are, of course, much older than Christianity itself.[37] We could equally note the continued existence of cults such as the Jehovah's Witnesses and the Mormons. Furthermore, if one follows Gamaliel's own example of Judas to its logical conclusion, even a movement's apparent disappearance can provide no concrete evidence that it is not from God, since it may reappear at a future date!

(2) Martin Luther

Another theologian who has used the Gamaliel principle positively is Martin Luther. He used it in two ways: in relation to the discernment of contemporary prophecy and also in a more general 'prophetic' sense.

Following the Diet of Worms, at which his work was condemned as heretical by the Imperial authorities, Luther

---

[36] Y. Yadin, *Masada: Herod's Fortress and the Zealots' Last Stand*, p. 199.

[37] 'Why My Name is Not Gamaliel', p. 8.

disappeared into hiding. Whilst he was in hiding a group of prophets from Zwickau came to his home town of Wittenberg, claiming to have received direct revelations from God. Without Luther's support, Philip Melanchthon dithered as to how he should respond to these prophets. Luther advised him in a letter: 'First of all, since they bear witness to themselves, one need not immediately accept them; according to John's counsel (1 John 4:1), the spirits are to be tested. If you cannot test them then you have the advice of Gamaliel that you postpone judgement.'[38]

Luther suggests that Melanchthon should begin his testing of the prophets by concentrating on their individual experiences of Christian life:

> You should enquire whether they have experienced spiritual distress and the divine birth, death and hell. If you should hear that all [their experiences] are pleasant, quiet, devout (as they say), and spiritual, then don't approve of them, even if they should say that they were caught up to the third heaven. The sign of the Son of Man is then missing, [i.e. the cross], which is the only touchstone of Christians and a certain differentiator between the spirits.[39]

In the same spirit, he concludes: 'Examine them and do not even listen if they speak of the glorified Jesus, unless you have first heard of the crucified Jesus.'[40]

What can we make of Luther's use of Gamaliel here ? Firstly, he has combined the words of Gamaliel with the idea of testing the spirits found in 1 John 4:1; if one cannot test them, take Gamaliel's advice. Significantly, Luther does not suggest that Melanchthon should leave them alone, waiting and seeing, and then acknowledging that if they are not overthrown then they are from God. Rather he asks for a rigorous test procedure against the prophets with a view to possibly banning their preaching completely. It appears Luther believed Gamaliel's advice should not be accepted as a substitute for testing the spirits, but regarded it as a useful and truthful option if one is

[38] *Letters I*, pp. 365–6.
[39] Ibid. p. 366.
[40] Ibid. p. 367.

unable to test the spirits. According to Gamaliel's measure, such spirits will either be overthrown or succeed.

Our discussion of Origen has shown that Melanchthon would need to wait for a very long time indeed before Gamaliel's principle would make it possible for him to *know* that a prophet was from God. But in this usage, Gamaliel's principle is very clearly a last resort for Luther; the response of someone unable to test the prophets, and so was perhaps not intended as a primary means of determining whether or not they were from God.

Luther's second use of Gamaliel does, however, seem to demonstrate a belief that Gamaliel's words will serve to vindicate a work of God. On two occasions Luther is recorded as citing Gamaliel's words to the effect that if his own work was not of God it would fail, but that if it was of God then none could withstand it.[41] By invoking Gamaliel Luther is doing two things: first, he is speaking prophetically against the imperial and papal authorities and warning them not to 'fight against God'; secondly, he is drawing comfort from the knowledge that what is of God will succeed against all human opposition. This idea is found elsewhere in the Bible; for example, in Isaiah 8:10: 'Take counsel together, but it will come to naught; speak a word, but it will not stand, for God is with us.'

Similarly, Romans 8:31: 'If God is for us, who is against us?' But would Luther be correct in seeing in Gamaliel's words a guarantee that his own work of God would succeed ? This is a frequent assumption (cf e.g. John Noble on p. 88 above). But this understanding is deeply flawed, and once again the flaw has to do with time. Certainly Christian theology is predicated upon the view that God's plan will succeed and that all humanity's plans against him will fail. But this is an eschatological truth — only at the end of history will it be vindicated (however that end is understood).[42] It is simply not true that every work of God succeeds in the present and that every merely human venture fails. Christians may take comfort in knowing that

---

[41] See *Psalms III*, p. 67; *Career of the Reformer II*, p. 121.

[42] See also Masters, 'Beware of the Counsel of Gamaliel', p. 12, and John Stott's words in the introductory section.

finally God will triumph but that assurance provides no guarantee that what one does for God, even as a genuine act of obedience in a genuine work of the Spirit, will result in success as Gamaliel defines it. That servants of God may suffer, fail and even die without seeing their stand for God vindicated in history is clear from numerous New Testament passages (Acts 7:54–60; 9:16; 12:2; Rom. 8:18; 2 Cor. 11:23–27; 12:7; 2 Thess. 1:5; 1 Pet. 2:20f; 4:19; 5:9). Modern examples might be the members of the confessing church in pre-war Germany, killed in Nazi concentration camps, or Oscar Romero, Archbishop of San Salvador, murdered on the 24th March 1980. Most poignant of all are the many who have faithfully given their lives and are known only to God.

What then of those who, like Luther, speak with a prophetic voice against the authorities? Unlike a prophetic pronouncement of judgment, this use of the principle can also only be understood eschatologically. It is not true that authorities will always fail to stop a movement of God. Again the authorities against whom Romero (and many other martyrs during this century) have prophesied may provide a sad example of this. Luther's use of the Gamaliel principle may provide eschatological hope for the Christian and perhaps cause repentance amongst the authorities, but that is all. Luther's application of the Gamaliel principle to himself can only be seen as a form of rhetoric!

(3) Jonathan Edwards

Our final example of a theologian using the Gamaliel principle is Jonathan Edwards (1703–1758). In 1741, during a time of revival in New England, Edwards published a three-part work entitled *The Distinguishing Marks of a Work of the Spirit of God.*[43] Part I listed fallacious marks which were used to argue something was not of the Spirit. Part II contains scriptural evidences for distinguishing a work of the Spirit of God. Here Edwards argues that these marks can distinguish a work of the Spirit from the work of Satan 'as an angel of light'.[44]

[43] In *On Revival* (1741), pp. 75–147.
[44] Ibid. pp. 109–20.

Having defined these marks Edwards draws some inferences from them in the final section. The first inference was that current events in New England were of the Spirit.[45] His second inference begins:

> Let us all be hence warned, by no means to oppose, or do any thing in the least to clog or hinder the work; but, on the contrary, to do our utmost to promote it. Now Christ is come down from Heaven in a remarkable and wonderful work of his Spirit, it becomes all his professed disciples to acknowledge him, and give him honour.[46]

After discussing the failure of the Jews to acknowledge Jesus and the works of the Spirit at Pentecost, Edwards addresses what he sees as the parallel failure amongst the ministers of the church of his day, those who are failing to recognize the Spirit of God, who are 'prudently' keeping silent and who are, in some cases, claiming to await the issue (fruits) of the work. For Edwards, their prudence in avoiding commenting on this clear work of the Spirit is, in fact, a secret kind of opposition to God which really hinders the work. Further, those who await the issue of the movement will await a clear sign in vain, as the Jews did, always seeking further signs. Edwards marvels that those pretending prudence in this way so easily pass up what he terms 'the most precious opportunity of obtaining divine light, grace, and comfort, heavenly and eternal benefits that God ever gave in New England',[47] having made no attempt to see for themselves.

Some people, however, have spoken contemptuously of the work in New England. They would have done better, says Edwards, to have learnt prudence from an unbelieving Jew, Gamaliel, and he cites Gamaliel's advice for them. They should not 'oppose [the work in New England], or say anything which has even an indirect tendency to bring it into discredit, lest they be found opposers of the Holy Spirit'.[48] Those who speak contemptuously of the work are one step from the unforgivable sin;

---

[45] Ibid. pp. 121–30.
[46] Ibid. p. 130.
[47] Ibid. p. 134.
[48] Ibid. p. 134.

that step being to call the work Satanic against their inward conviction that it is of the Holy Spirit.[49]

There are at least two problems with Edwards's use of Gamaliel here. The first is the historical problem already outlined. The scoffers may take Edwards's advice to keep quiet and so avoid the risk (?) of blaspheming the Spirit, but discover Gamaliel's principle will tell them nothing about the origin of the New England revival. But Edwards also appears to be guilty of a gross contradiction. It is impossible to reconcile his advice to the scoffers to be prudent like Gamaliel with his condemnation of those 'prudent' men who are keeping quiet about the present work of the Spirit. In Acts, Gamaliel's advice is not to make one's mind up about whether or not a work is of the Spirit, but rather that no decision is necessary at all, ever. Such an attitude would surely be condemned by Edwards, who insists: 'Now Christ is come down from Heaven in a remarkable and wonderful work of his spirit, *it becomes all his professed disciples to acknowledge him and give him honour*.'[50] Gamaliel, then, should actually be Edwards's prime target, on account of his own refusal to recognize the words of the apostles as God's prophetic voice!

Sadly, however, this is in effect the advice of Mark Stibbe and others to those who would question the Toronto Blessing. Questioning Christians should stand back, wait, *never* learn whether a movement is from God or not, and thus merit the condemnation pronounced by Edwards upon such indecision — should they not have acknowledged the Spirit of God ?

4. The Meaning of Acts 5

In the light of all of these positive views of Gamaliel, it is time to look at the text of Acts, and ask, why is Gamaliel seen so

---

[49] This step seems to me a large one; those who condemn a movement in all sincerity are a long way from those who condemn a movement whilst knowing it is from the Holy Spirit. It is also noteworthy that Mark Stibbe's exegesis on the blasphemy against the Spirit misses this point altogether; according to him, one need only condemn a movement of the Spirit to be in danger. whether one knows it is of the Spirit or not (*Refreshing*, pp. 173–80).

[50] Edwards, *On Revival*, p. 130.

positively by Christians? Why does he tempt them into what appears to be so dangerous a path? The answer to these questions is not difficult but it has profound consequences for Christians as they read the book of Acts. The reason why Gamaliel's principle is so attractive is that Luke himself uses the words of Gamaliel positively in Acts 5 in order to proclaim both the God-given nature of the Christian Gospel and to present the apostles as the true leaders of Israel. At the same time, the words of Gamaliel and the response of the Sanhedrin function negatively and serve to discredit the old leadership of Israel completely.

It was of the greatest importance to Luke that he demonstrate to his readers that God is faithful to his promises. How else could they have 'security' in their faith (Luke 1:4)? He achieved his purpose by depicting the early church as a new Israel — the proper recipient of the blessings promised to Abraham (Luke 1:72; Acts 3:25; 7:8), which included those of the old Israel who had received Jesus (Luke 2:25–32, 37). The choosing of Matthias as the twelfth of 'the Twelve' (Acts 1:15–26) demonstrates the importance of having their numbers match the highly symbolic twelve tribes of Israel, and implies for Luke that these men form the nucleus of Israel and constitute its leadership.

As Acts progresses Luke begins to show how the early church came to expand. The life of the church begins with three thousand converts on the Day of Pentecost (2:41), and Luke outlines their fellowship (2:42–47; 4:23–36), the healing and preaching ministry of the apostles (3:1–26; 5:12–16), and their first brush with the leaders of Israel (4:1–21). The story of Ananias and Sapphira in Acts 5:1–11 conclusively demonstrates the authority of the apostles within the church. This is followed by Luke's description of a second appearance before the Sanhedrin in which the authority of the apostles over the Israel of God is confirmed through the words of Gamaliel and the response of the Sanhedrin. Gamaliel himself, this respected teacher of Israel, utters the truth that Luke wants his readers to hear; that the church will not be overthrown, and that the leadership of Israel, which has refused to listen to Jesus, has been put aside. The expansion of the church is then given a powerful impetus with the death of Stephen and the subsequent persecution under Saul, which scatters the church to 'all Judea and Samaria, and to the ends of the earth' (Acts 1:8).

However, it is important to note that this positive use of Gamaliel's words operates on an ironic level. Gamaliel himself is unaware of the significance of his own words and is himself thoroughly discredited by them. Luke's intended irony becomes clear when one recognizes the importance of Peter's statements in Acts 4:19–20 and 5:29; namely, that he and John must obey God rather than men, that is, Israel's discredited leaders. L.T Johnson puts it like this:

> Gamaliel's advice about this 'plan or work' is really an example of bad faith. He is (in the sense Luke uses the term of the Pharisees and teachers of the law), a hypocrite, for he wants to appear righteous, and he has all the right convictions, but he will not respond to the prophetic call before him. Like the Pharisees and teachers of the Law in Luke 7:29 he 'rejects God's plan'.[51]

Similarly, when the time comes for the Sanhedrin to make a decision about what to do with Peter and John, they obey a man, Gamaliel, rather than the voice of God delivered by the apostles (5:40). At this point the Sanhedrin, who are the very first to take Gamaliel's advice, also immediately find themselves 'fighting against God'. Their reward (and Gamaliel's) is spelled out in the prophetic words of Peter in Acts 3:23: 'Anyone who does not listen to him [Jesus] will be completely cut off from among his people.'

Because Gamaliel's statement is ironic, there also is some truth implied within it. Luke's Christian readers will obviously see the situation of the fledgling Christian movement truthfully mirrored in the words of Gamaliel. It is not surprising, therefore, that this validation of some truth within the statement is transferred to the statement as a whole within its present context. It is this transference, I believe, that may well be responsible for the numerous positive assessments of

---

[51] *Acts*, p. 103.

Gamaliel, ultimately moving him into the Christian camp itself.[52]

However, it is here that an illegitimate move is being made. Luke's perspective on these words is quite different from that intended by Gamaliel. For Luke, the words show that the Christian movement itself, the new Israel, will not be overthrown. Luke's positive use of Gamaliel's words is a general eschatological one that is not demonstrable in history. This is a truth known to his readers only by faith, as one cannot prove empirically that something will last forever. As we noted earlier in our discussion of Luther, it is only at the end of history that God will see the Christian movement itself vindicated.[53]

---

[52] According to some, for example, the Pharisees (and hence Gamaliel) should be seen as getting a very good press in Luke-Acts; thus Krodel notes that they are absent from the passion narrative of Luke, and states without any explanatory comment that it is the 'Sadducees' who are found to oppose God in Acts 5 (p. 129). However, Luke's presentation is not really as positive as such commentators would have us believe. Although the Pharisees are not mentioned by name in Luke's passion narrative, the Sanhedrin is! Since Luke specifically identifies Gamaliel as a member of the Sanhedrin (Acts 5:34), and since, according to Luke, the trial of Jesus took place during the daytime when the full complement of the Sanhedrin would presumably have been there, Gamaliel should surely be seen as one of those who was present at the condemnation of Jesus. He had also met Peter and John before in Acts 4 (cf. 4:15), seen the man healed by them (Acts 4:14), and heard Peter declare that it was by the name of Jesus whom 'you [the Sanhedrin] crucified . . . that this man stands before you healed' (Acts 4:10). Similarly, those who are found to be opposing God at the conclusion of Acts 5 are the whole Sanhedrin, who all agree to accept Gamaliel's advice, and not just the Sadducees. Does the fact that the word 'Pharisee' is not mentioned until Acts 5:34 allow us to see them as good in Luke's eyes? See also Johnson, *Acts*, pp. 99–103.

[53] We need not enquire here into Luke's eschatological perspective. His work includes two kinds of texts which witness either to the closeness of the parousia and judgment (Jesus' return; Luke 3:9; 18:7–8; 21:31–2) or to its being delayed (Luke 12:45; 19:11). Dale Allison suggests that Acts 1:7 sums up Luke's position: 'It is not for you to know the times or dates the Father has set by his own authority.' ('Eschatology' in *The Dictionary of Jesus and the Gospels*, pp. 206–9; cf. p. 209.) In Acts itself this eschatology is, not unnaturally, in the background; Luke is after all concerned with describing the historical spread of the church. But in Acts 5 Gamaliel's statement is given its true perspective only in the light of Luke's theme of the church as Israel and of his eschatology.

The first important point is thus that Luke does not intend to offer in Gamaliel's words the proposition that every individual doing God's work or every individual movement of God will succeed. The numerous accounts in Acts of the punishment and death of individuals and the failure of attempts to preach in particular cities make this abundantly clear. Stephen is stoned to death (7:60). James, the brother of John, is killed by Herod (12:2). Paul and Barnabas flee from Iconium (14:6). Paul is stoned at Lystra, and thrown out of the city (14:19). Paul and Silas are beaten and jailed in Philippi, before leaving the city (16:22–3, 40).

The second key point to consider concerning Luke's appropriation of the Gamaliel principle is the way in which he avoids the difficulty we saw in Origen — the impossibility of proving historically that a movement has been overthrown. Luke achieves this by implying the overthrow of the old leadership of Israel has already taken place *prophetically* even if not historically. The failure of Gamaliel and the Sanhedrin to listen to the apostles has placed them under Peter's prophetic condemnation in Acts 3:23, and thus, while not historically overthrown, they have been prophetically 'cut off from among [Jesus'] people,' the new people of God, the new Israel.

Thus it is clear that Luke appropriates Gamaliel's words in the only legitimate way in which they can be used; namely, eschatologically. But this validation must not be transferred to Gamaliel's own use of the principle as a historical measure. To do so is to fall into the snares evident in the work of Origen, Luther and Edwards. It is impossible for humanity to state unequivocally that any movement is overthrown or has succeeded, and it is blatantly untrue that such historical success or failure would have any bearing upon whether or not a particular movement was from God. This calls into serious question the use of the Gamaliel principle as a means of deferring judgment by a movement which claims the attention of Christian churches. Adhering to the Gamaliel principle will tell us nothing. The only possible consequence will be either that we withhold our support from a movement of God and thus hinder it (incurring Edwards' wrath), or else we allow the churches to be harmed by false teaching and practices.

5. Objections

In this final section I shall attempt to outline more systematically the theological reasons why Gamaliel's principle is unacceptable as it is commonly used. This argument is based largely upon the work of the Dutch theologian, G.C. Berkouwer, and his discussion of Gamaliel in *The Providence of God*.[54]

In order to understand Berkouwer's objections to a positive use of Gamaliel's words one initially needs to understand the distinction between a pure and a mixed article of faith. This distinction, a common one in dogmatics, concerns the question of whether an article of faith can be known apart from the Scriptures. In this case Berkouwer argues that the providence of God cannot be deduced through natural theology; it is a 'pure article', which can be known only from the special revelation of the Scriptures.[55] The fallen nature of humanity, he argues, does not allow us to read from the events of history what God is doing; any attempt to do so becomes an arbitrary one in which views of God's Providence are developed according to one's concept of God. Without Christ, Berkouwer argues, these views are based upon idols.[56]

In contrast, the Christian doctrine of Providence, drawn from the Scriptures, provides an understanding of God's overall sustenance and government of the world.[57] By this revelation the Christian confesses in faith that God's providence is total, for the Father in heaven 'causes his sun to rise on the evil and the good, and sends rain on the righteous and the unrighteous' (Matt. 5:45); nothing occurs apart from Divine providence, not even the falling to the ground of a single sparrow (Matt. 10:29). History in its totality is all part of the one work of God, the central event of which is the cross of Christ.[58]

However, a problem arises here for Berkouwer in the relationship between God's overall and total providence and attempts to discern 'God's finger', the special intervention of God in [the]

[54] *Studies in Dogmatics.*
[55] Ibid. p. 44.
[56] Ibid. pp. 45–6.
[57] Ibid. pp. 50–124.
[58] Ibid. pp. 177–8.

(usually) extra-ordinary acts in history. These attempts to define what is often called 'special providence' become especially problematic when these historical events are designated as being of God and history as a whole is then interpreted in the light of them. Berkouwer's exemplar of the problem is the rise of Hitler and the Christians who saw in his success a revelation of the will of God and therefore supported him. The 'German Christians' saw in this event the finger of God pointing out the 'true' destiny of Germany and, as Berkouwer puts it, 'a fragment of history was in effect canonized as a new revelation'.[59] The problem is that the interpretation of such a historical event as a special revelation too easily becomes a 'piously disguised form of self-justification'.[60] Such an interpretation, with this faulty understanding of providence, leaves those who practise it with a subjective judgment in which they can only utilize what Berkouwer describes as 'religious intuition or divination'.[61]

This flawed understanding of providence also contravenes Berkouwer's insistence that the doctrine of providence be a pure article of faith. His theological reasoning here is simple:

1) No-one can recognize God's finger without knowing him.
2) Therefore facts and events can be seen and understood only in the light of biblical revelation.
3) We thus have no way of understanding history as a second independent source of revelation.[62]

Jesus' comments in Luke 13:1–5 about the Galileans killed by Pilate and the tower that fell in Siloam warn us against drawing conclusions about 'events' since they show that Jesus himself rejected common interpretations which saw these historical events as revealing God's purpose.[63]

If one cannot discern the will of God directly from the events of history, then the question arises as to whether or not there is any way of seeing how God is at work in history to achieve

[59] Ibid. p. 162.
[60] Ibid. p. 166.
[61] Ibid. p. 171.
[62] Ibid. pp. 170–1.
[63] Ibid. pp. 171–2.

his purposes or of sensing the leading of God within the life of the Christian. According to Berkouwer, there is. What Christians can and must do is to interpret events using scriptural revelation thus removing the arbitrariness of their interpretations. There can be no proceeding from historical facts isolated from faith in the revelation of God through Jesus Christ. As Berkouwer puts it:

> [w]e shall never recognize God's finger in history without first meeting him in the fulness of his revelation. This denies us the luxury of simple conclusions, of the ability to perceive the finger of God in events which we arbitrarily select. We must constantly judge ourselves whether we are subjecting our thinking to the norm [i.e. Scripture] which is established for all explanation of all events.[64]

In other words, we can say of God's working in history only what a faithful holistic reading of Scripture allows us to say.

In his discussion of Gamaliel and his principle, Berkouwer quotes the words of the Dutch statesman and theologian Abraham Kuyper:

> Gamaliel's advice is bad. It is not true that God destroys forthwith that which is not from him and crowns with success every endeavour of his believers . . . How is it that Gamaliel's advice, so profoundly untrue, is repeated again and again in life? Could it not be just as well the other way around, that to have no success suggests virtue? Is the cross a mark of holy origin? Oppressed, downtrodden, molested — can these not be signs that you are walking on the way of God?[65]

Gamaliel's failure is, according to Berkouwer, caused by his seeing the overthrowing of Theudas and Judas as sources of independent knowledge concerning God's will and

[64] Ibid. p. 179, used with permission of the Publishers, Eerdmans.

[65] Ibid. p. 173.

[66] It is important to note that independence here does not mean a total independence from the Scriptures; one is culpable if one's theology is such that historical events are understood as sources of revelation on the basis of a deficient theology, and thus are 'independent' of the full revelation of the Scriptures.

purposes.[66] Gamaliel's error is that he believes *on the basis of his own prior theological understanding* that these events will tell him of the place of these movements within the will of God. His theological understanding is at fault because it does not take account of the 'fullness' revealed in the Hebrew Scriptures; it is based upon a false and partial theology of success which implicitly denies the Scripture's witness to the theology of suffering and, in the case of Christians, to the theology of the cross.

Finally, and lest we charismatics believe that Berkouwer's critique of Gamaliel does not apply to us, it should also be noted that charismatically derived events and their interpretation are also subject to the same strictures as the interpretation of historical events; prophecies need to be tested against Scripture. This point has often been obscured in charismatic churches, prophecy being seen implicitly if not explicitly by some as being on a par with the Scriptures.[67] But as Stanley Porter puts it in referring to some of the phenomena of the Toronto blessing:

> Those who would attribute the same level of authority as the Bible to these supposed revelations have accepted some concept of an open canon, perhaps without realising it. The vast mainstream of orthodox Christianity throughout most of its history has held to the concept of a closed canon. I would argue that this was for good reasons. The alternative is a canon with flexible boundaries, subject to expansion (and potentially subtraction). But a set of logical and theological questions are raised by this. How does one judge which new revelations should be included? What happens if a new revelation contradicts previous revelation? Should the old revelation be discarded or do we introduce blatant contradictions into the Scriptures, and how do we decide which one to follow

[67] David Pawson, for example, sees 'an overemphasis on immediate revelation [leading] progressively to three distorted views on prophecy, each more dangerous than the last.' The first is that of seeing a prophecy as an addition to scripture; the second is to see prophecy as an alternative to scripture; the third is to see prophecy as an advance on scripture, *The Fourth Wave*, p. 79.

in future circumstances? What does this imply about the traditional understanding of God and his knowledge and power? If the new revelation introduces only material that supports previous revelation, why is this revelation necessary? It is reassuring to see that most of those writing on the Toronto Blessing are not heading down this path.[68]

6. Conclusion

If one accepts Berkouwer's view of Divine providence, Gamaliel's fault, shared by all promoters of his principle, is their common belief that a particular historical event — the success or failure of a plan or movement — would reveal God's purpose. Gamaliel believed that the overthrow of Theudas and Judas demonstrated that they were not from God; Origen believed that Jesus was proved Son of God by the historical failure of other pretenders; Luther believed that his own work of God could not be overthrown; Edwards also believed that if the movement in New England was of God it could not be overthrown, as also did Watson of the charismatic movement; Noble believed that the success of his church would show that God was behind it; Pender, Roberts and Stibbe (and many others) all believe that the success or failure of the Toronto Blessing will show whether it is of God or not. These things were and are believed despite the clear witness of Scripture that God's providence covers all peoples, making the success or failure of a given movement a troublesome criterion. Even the Christian Gospel itself cannot be vindicated on these grounds apart from faith in the promises of God. Furthermore, the Christian life involves failure and death as well as success and honour. A theology of the cross is at least as, if not much more important than a theology of glory!

---

[68] 'Shaking the Biblical Foundations', in *The Toronto Blessing — or Is It?*, pp. 38–65; see pp. 60–1. The position outlined here should not be seen as that of a cessationist. I have no difficulty with the ongoing use of charismata within the church. But I believe it is necessary to hold this together with the concept of the canon and that many failings of the charismatic movement can be traced to a failure to do just this.

It seems clear that the Gamaliel principle does not work as a means of deciding whether or not something is from God, and that there are sound reasons — historical, logical, textual, and theological — why this is so. Set within the context of a Christian view of providence, Gamaliel's principle is purely and simply an arbitrary construction of biblical material which, in his context, is untrue. If this judgment is correct, then we now need to turn, unhindered by rhetoric about Gamaliel's principle, to the questions currently being asked concerning an appropriate response to the Toronto Blessing and similar movements. Two groups are being wrongly advised. Questioning Christians wonder why they are so unable to test this movement that they should have to wait like Gamaliel. And those who are being encouraged to engage fully in the Blessing need to know whether they should really become part of a movement which cannot (apparently) be fully tested, especially in cases where the price appears to be a destruction of their fellowships and the alienation of many other Christians.

7. Postscript

After I had finished the bulk of the work for this essay, I was discussing Gamaliel and his principle with a friend who is involved in a pro-Toronto church. He readily confirmed that his church had invoked Gamaliel's principle when first deciding to go with the Blessing. However, in recent days the Blessing meetings had become less well attended, to the point that questions were being asked, and accusations made. It seems that those who had once used Gamaliel so positively and had agreed that if the Blessing were to fail it was because it was human in origin rather than of God were now blaming the failure of Toronto meetings on those in the church who lacked commitment.

Apparently a further problem with Gamaliel's principle has surfaced. Even if the principle were true, people would, it appears, still not believe it, preferring instead to blame a movement's failure on others. If they had paid more attention to Gamaliel they would have remembered that, according to him, if the Movement were of God it could not fail! However, since I have argued that Gamaliel's principle cannot be used in such a fashion, it follows that the failure of Toronto meetings (if that is what is happening) has no bearing at all upon the origin of the Toronto Blessing. At the very worst, what may be happening is the failure of a work of God because of the false rhetoric of its proponents and the reluctance of the Christians whom they have alienated to get involved in the Movement.

Bibliography

Allison, D., 'Eschatology', in *The Dictionary of Jesus and the Gospels* eds. J.B. Green, S. McKnight, I.H. Marshall (Leicester: IVP, 1992), 206–9

Berkouwer, G.C., *The Providence of God. Studies in Dogmatics* (Grand Rapids: Eerdmans, 1952)

Bruce, F.F., *Acts of the Apostles*, NICNT (Grand Rapids: Eerdmans, 1985)

Chilton, B., 'Gamaliel', in *Anchor Bible Dictionary*, Vol II (New York: Doubleday, 1992), 904–6

Chrysostom, John, *Homilies on Acts and Romans*. Nicene and Post-Nicene Fathers, 1st series, Vol XI (Edinburgh: T and T Clark, 1889)

'The Clementine Recognitions', in *Tatian, Theophilus, and the Clementine Recognitions*, Ante-nicene Christian Library, Vol III (Edinburgh: T and T Clark, no date), 1: lv–lxxii, 179–90

Edwards, J., 'The Distinguishing Marks of a Work of the Spirit of God', in *On Revival* (1741) (Edinburgh: Banner of Truth, 1965), 75–147

Ferris, T., *Acts*. Interpreter's Bible Commentary (Nashville: Abingdon, 1954)

Gigot, F.E., 'Gamaliel', in *The Catholic Encyclopaedia*, Vol. 6, *Fathers to Gregory* (London: 1909), 374–5

Henry, Matthew, *A Commentary on the Old and New Testaments*, Vol. III (London: 1883)

Hewitt. B., 'John Noble', in *Doing a New Thing* (London: Hodder and Stoughton, 1995)

Johnson, L.T., *Acts*. Sacra Pagina, Vol. 5 (Minnesota: The Liturgical Press, 1992)

Krodel, G.A., *Acts*. Augsburg Commentary (Minneapolis: Fortress, 1986)
Luther, Martin, *Letters I*, Luther's Works, Vol 48 (Philadelphia: Fortress, 1963)
—, *Psalms III*, Luther's Works, Vol 14 (Philadelphia: Fortress, 1958)
—, *Career of the Reformer II*, Luther's Works Vol 32 (Philadelphia: Fortress, 1958)
Masters. P., 'Beware of the Counsel of Gamaliel', *Sword and Trowel*, (1995) no. 3, pp. 11–13
Origen, *Origen: Contra Celsum* (trans. H. Chadwick; Cambridge: Cambridge University Press, 1953)
Pawson, D., *The Fourth Wave: Charismatics and Evangelicals, Are We Ready to come Together?* (London: Hodder and Stoughton, 1992)
Porter, S., 'Shaking the Biblical Foundations', in *The Toronto Blessing — or Is It?* eds. S.E. Porter and P.J. Richter (London: DLT, 1995), 38–65
Roberts, D., *The 'Toronto Blessing'*, (Eastbourne: Kingsway Publications, 1994)
Schleiermacher, F., 'A Sermon on Gamaliel', in *Sämmtliche Werke* 2: *Predigten* Vol III (Berlin, 1834 f.), p. 300
Schürer. E., *The History of the Jewish People in the Age of Jesus Christ*, Vol II (rev ed) eds. Vermes, Miller, and Black, (Edinburgh: T and T Clark, 1979)
Smail. T., 'Why My Name is Not Gamaliel', *Church of England Newspaper*, (Friday, Feb 3, 1995), p. 8
Stibbe, M., 'Four Waves of the Spirit', *Skepsis*, (Summer 1995), pp. 6–8
—, *Times of Refreshing: A Practical Theology of Revival for Today* (London: Marshall Pickering, 1995), pp. 6–8
Stott, J., *Acts*. The Bible Speaks Today (Leicester: IVP, 1990)
Watson, D., *Discipleship* (London: Hodder and Stoughton, 1981)
Williams. D.J., *Acts*, NIBC (Peabody, Mass: Hendrickson, 1985)
Yadin, Y., *Masada: Herod's Fortress and the Zealots' Last Stand* (London: Weidenfeld and Nicolson, 1966)

Hypnosis, Healing and the Christian
John Court

Hypnosis is a controversial practice with many myths about its power and dangers. *Hypnosis, Healing and the Christian* cuts through the confusion to present a balanced defence of the use of hypnosis by Christians, arguing that it is 'a powerful tool in bringing about psychological change'

Court avoids minimising the dangers of this powerful phenomenon as he discusses examples of clinical hypnosis by Christians who have found emotional and spiritual benefits from its use. Setting ethical concerns about the use of hypnosis firmly within a framework of the biblical material, he argues that hypnosis is a morally neutral technique which may be used for good or ill. Its use by pagan and other religions should not prevent its constructive and godly use by Christians.

This stimulating book will be of interest not only to those involved in counselling and healing ministries but also to Christians interested in a broader understanding of how our human minds work.

"John Court has done it again. He has taken a problematic treatment and made it palatable for the Christian . . . He does not see hypnosis as always helpful but he does present this powerful tool as helping Christians live up to their intentions. I recommend it to all – clients and counsellors alike!"
H. Newton Malony, Senior Professor of Psychology, Fuller Theological Seminary

John Court is Director of Counselling at Tabor College in Adelaide, Australia. He has written a number of books including *Pornography: A Christian Critique* (Paternoster Press) and *Rainbows through the Rain* (Lutheran Publishing House).

0-85364-802-6

Baptism, Reconciliation and Unity
Kevin Roy

This stimulating book argues that although baptism is of great importance to the church, differing views about the mode and subjects of baptism are not of such weight that they justify division between denominations.

"As one who has spent much time in producing literature that concentrates on the rights and wrongs of the Church's interpretations of baptism I find myself in agreement with Dr. Roy, and commend his book to the careful study of the reader."
George R. Beasley-Murray, Author of *Baptism in the New Testament* (Paternoster Press)

"In this book we have an approach that is in the very best sense of the word evangelical ecumenical theology . . . The evangelical world should consider the appeal of this book very, very seriously."
Adrio König

"This is an impassioned but scholarly plea for mutual understanding amongst Christians, at a point where division does great harm to the cause of Mission . . . A clear-sighted book, marked by Christian charity, a concern for Truth, and a love for Christ's Gospel . . . I recommend it highly."
Donald Bridge, Author of *The Water that Divide*s (with David Phypers) and a retired Baptist minister.

Kevin Roy is Lecturer at the Baptist Theological College, Cape Town and is a Baptist Minister.

0-85364-815-8

Church Planting: Laying Foundations

Stuart Murray

Church planting in back in vogue in Britain at the end of the twentieth century. Although church attendance is still in decline, new churches are being planted and church planting strategies have been adopted by several denominations.

But do we really need more churches? What kinds of churches are being planted? Where are they being planted? Is church planting an effective mission strategy?

Stuart Murray identifies some of the theological and strategic issues which need to be addressed if contemporary church planting is to be built on firm foundations. Drawing on a wide range of reading, this book asks radical questions and encourages church planters to think through and articulate a theological framework for their activities. It warns against establishing clones of existing churches and resists making church planting an end in itself.

This is a book for practitioners, but for practitioners who are prepared to think, and who are willing to ask searching questions about the kinds of churches needed in a post-Christian and post-modern culture.

"Page after page makes us think. The range of issues keep us on our toes . . . I am convinced that we shall all be in Stuart Murray's debt for the way he has written to provoke such thought and action."
From the foreword by Michael Quicke, Principal of Spurgeon's College.

Dr. Stuart Murray has been involved in church planting for the past twenty years. He lectures at Spurgeon's College where he is Oasis Director of Church Planting and Evangelism. His previous works include *The Challenge of the City* and *Explaining Church Discipline*.

0-85364-825-5

Changing Values

How to Find Moral Truth in Modern Times

David Attwood

"David Attwood exposes the superficiality of much contemporary talk about 'values' . . . He argues that moral rules, far from being irrelevant in today's climate, are still essential and can be framed in such a way that avoids the extremes of legalism and moralism . . . Working on a variety of issues, he satisfyingly links creation and covenant as the coherent basis of Christian ethics, and shows how both flow into the ethical motivation of the Kingdom of God."
Rev. Dr. Chris Wright, All Nations Christian College

"David Attwood offers a clear and coherent approach to moral theory derived from Christian faith. Drawing on the theology of Karl Barth, Paul Ramsey and others, Attwood argues that faithful love is the centre, seen in the character of God the creator, in God's covenant relationship with his world, in the practice of forgiveness, and especially in love's concern for the weak and vulnerable."
David Atkinson, the Archdeacon of Lewisham

Addressing specific issues including property, parenthood and euthanasia, *Changing Values* explains how an understanding of creation and covenant love can give firm foundations for moral truth, confident to withstand moral confusion and cynicism.

This book builds at a more popular level on the foundations laid by Oliver O'Donovan's grounding of Christian ethics in the biblical affirmation of creation.

David Attwood is Lecturer in Christian Ethics and Director of Studies at Trinity College Bristol. He has also written *Paul Ramsey's Political Ethics* (Rowman and Littlefield 1992)

0-85364-806-9